PASSPORT TO AMC'S

HIGH HUTS

IN THE WHITE MOUNTAINS

Ty Wivell

Appalachian Mountain Club Books
Boston, Massachusetts

AMC is a nonprofit organization and sales of AMC Books fund our mission of protecting the Northeast outdoors. If you appreciate our efforts and would like to make a donation to AMC, contact us at Appalachian Mountain Club, 5 Joy Street, Boston, MA 02108.
www.outdoors.org/publications/books/

Distributed by The Globe Pequot Press, Guilford, Connecticut.

Library of Congress Cataloging-in-Publication Data
Wivell, Ty.
  Passport to AMC's high huts of the White Mountains / Ty Wivell.
    p. cm.
  Includes bibliographical references.
  ISBN 978-1-934028-49-0 (alk. paper)
 1. Hiking—White Mountains (N.H. and Me.)—Guidebooks. 2. Hiking—Appalachian Trail—Guidebooks. 3. Huts--White Mountains (N.H. and Me.)—Guide
books. 4. Huts—Appalachian Trail—Guidebooks. 5. White Mountains (N.H. and Me.)—Guidebooks. 6. Appalachian trail—Guidebooks. I. Title. II. Title: Passport to Appalachian Mountain Club's high huts of the White Mountains.
  GV199.42.W47W6 2011
  917.42'204--dc22
                                                          2010050763
The paper used in this publication meets the minimum requirements of the American National Standard for Information Sciences—Permanence of Paper for Printed Library Materials, ANSI Z39.48-1984.

Interior pages contain 30% post-consumer recycled fiber.
Cover contains 10% post-consumer recycled fiber.
Printed in the United States of America, using vegetable-based inks.

10 9 8 7 6 5 4 3 2 1   11 12 13 14 15 16

Contents

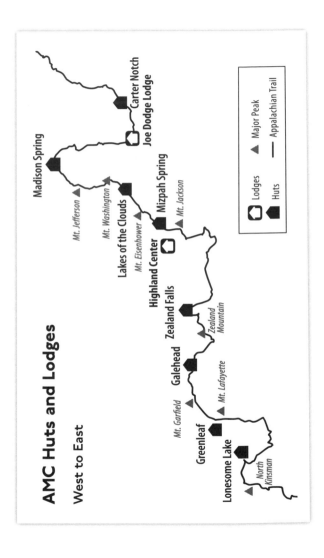

AMC Huts and Lodges

West to East

Carter Notch

Joe Dodge Lodge

Madison Spring

Mt. Jefferson

Mt. Washington

Mizpah Spring

Lakes of the Clouds

Mt. Eisenhower

Mt. Jackson

Highland Center

Zealand Falls

Zealand Mountain

Galehead

Mt. Garfield

Mt. Lafayette

Greenleaf

Lonesome Lake

North Kinsman

| Lodges | ■ Major Peak |
| Huts | — Appalachian Trail |

Essays

Appendices

Welcome

If I had to name the iconic experiences that represent what AMC is all about, our hut system would be high on the list. A hut is one place where all aspects of our mission—conservation, education, and recreation—come together. It is also a place where thousands of children and adults get their first real introduction to a "high mountain" experience in the Northeast.

Reading this book, you will quickly get a sense of the rich history and personalities that are part of AMC's hut system. Our first hut was designed to solve a particular problem, providing shelter to tired trampers or those seeking refuge in an emergency. Later on, meals were served to make it possible for hikers to travel light and still enjoy life above treeline. As the popularity of the hut experience grew and more huts were built, it became a system of eight huts, each a day's hike apart through the spectacular White Mountains.

Although the eighth hut was added in 1964, our hut system continues to evolve. In fact, the hut experience today is far different from that of a generation ago. Today our huts serve as models for environmental education and stewardship, showcasing sustainable practices such as use of alternative energy, waste reduction, and composting, and serving as focal points of our air quality and alpine ecosystem monitoring and research. Our goal is to make sure each hut guest walks away with an even greater understanding of the natural environment and how each guest can play a role in protecting it.

Of course, none of this could be achieved without the support of our outstanding crews and hut volunteers. Their energy and love of the outdoors are infectious. Many guests and visitors say their interaction with our hut crews is the most memorable part of their trip.

Whether you are a first-time visitor or longtime guest, you are part of the story of the high huts. On behalf of our dedicated staff and volunteers, welcome to AMC's huts.

Andy Falender

President
Appalachian Mountain Club

Acknowledgments

This project was charitably supported by friends, family, and colleagues who genuinely encouraged my efforts, always nurtured my inspiration, and patiently endured my absences.

At AMC, I would like to thank Heather Stephenson, publisher, for both supporting the idea and overseeing its ultimate completion. Many thanks to Athena Lakri, production manager, for her diligence in reviewing photos and guiding the book's design. I would also like to thank Kevin Breunig (vice president for communications and marketing) for his editorial contributions. I am particularly indebted to Becky Fullerton, AMC's librarian and archivist, for enthusiastically embracing the project and enduring my incessant inquiries. A special thank you to Kimberly Duncan-Mooney, AMC Books' project editor, who stepped into this project halfway down the trail with grace, good humor, and a keen eye for detail. I am exceedingly grateful to Jim Hamilton for sharing his wealth of knowledge and experience. And much appreciation to AMC Huts Manager Eric Pederson and Senior Naturalist Nancy Ritger for taking time out of their very busy schedules to share their insights. Above all, I want to thank the delightful AMC hut croos for graciously sharing their "summer homes" with me and providing the sustenance and enthusiasm that nourishes the hut system year after year.

I am deeply indebted to Andrea Greeley, who eagerly shared the trail with me and cheerfully endured the trials that accompanied this project. As always, thank you to my colleagues at Stoner-Andrews, Inc., for the latitude to pursue my outside interests. Finally, a deep, heartfelt thank you to my pal Cima, who could not accompany me on this latest adventure but is with me wherever I go.

Ty Wivell

hikeSafe

The U.S. Forest Service and New Hampshire Fish & Game Department have developed "hikeSafe," a program to encourage hiker responsibility in the White Mountain National Forest. The hikeSafe "Hiker Responsibility Code" states:

You are responsible for yourself, so be prepared:

- With knowledge and gear. Become self-reliant by learning about the terrain, conditions, local weather, and your equipment before you start.
- To leave your plans. Tell someone where you are going, the trails you are hiking, when you'll return, and your emergency plans.
- To stay together. When you start as a group, hike as a group, and end as a group. Pace your hike to the slowest person.
- To turn back. Weather changes quickly in the mountains. Fatigue and unexpected conditions can also affect your hike. Know your limitations and when to postpone your hike. The mountains will be there another day.
- For emergencies, even if you are headed out for just an hour. An injury, severe weather, or a wrong turn could become life threatening. Don't assume you will be rescued; know how to rescue yourself.
- To share the hiker code with others.

1

A Brief History

On January 8, 1876, 34 men gathered at the Massachusetts Institute of Technology (then in Boston) to discuss their shared interest in mountain exploration. Among the group were noted academics, including Edward C. Pickering, Thayer Professor of Physics at MIT, who had called the meeting, and Charles Hitchcock, New Hampshire's state geologist. The men talked about establishing an organization devoted to mountain study. Some advocated for a "New England Geographical Society," but, as one attendee later noted, "wiser councils prevailed." Instead of "one more learned society," the men decided upon "a vigorous, full-blooded, ardent club."

With that, the fledgling Appalachian Mountain Club (AMC) drew up a constitution and set forth its goal to "explore the mountains of New England and the adjacent regions, both for scientific and artistic purposes." The Club established five departments to achieve its primary ambitions: natural history, topography, art, exploration, and improvements. The latter department was designated for "building paths, camps, and other conveniences" and would soon provide the impetus for the first of the high huts.

AMC had been founded amid unprecedented interest in the White Mountains of New Hampshire. The arrival of the railroad in the latter half of the nineteenth century ushered in the so-called "Golden Age" of White Mountain tourism. Within a few decades, the region was transformed from a remote outpost to an enclave of extravagant resort hotels. Most catered to well-heeled travelers, eager to enjoy what was being coined as America's "most accessible wilderness."

In truth, there were less than a dozen paths to the major summits, and most of the attention was devoted to Mount Washington, the region's highest and most famous peak. Abel Crawford and his son, Ethan Allen Crawford, had blazed the first trail up the great mountain in 1819. In an effort to attract more tourists, Abel's son Thomas turned the trail into a bridle path in 1840. By 1853, the summit boasted two stone shelters, and plans were underway to construct a "Road to the Sky." The Mount Washington Carriage (now "Auto") Road was completed in 1861, the same year that New Hampshire native Sylvester Marsh was granted a patent for an "Inclined Railroad."

Marsh had visited Mount Washington in August 1857. Ascending Crawford Path on foot, he and his companion were nearly overtaken by high winds and freezing rain. When they finally reached the summit and the safety of the Tip-Top House, Marsh resolved to find a safer and easier way to scale the high peak. By 1869, his four-ton locomotive, *Peppersass,* reached the summit via the world's first mountain-climbing railroad. The Mount Washington Cog Railway was an immediate sensation and would soon be carrying thousands of visitors to the summit. To accommodate the multitudes, stone shelters were replaced by a massive two-and-a-half story hotel. When the Mount Washington Summit House opened in 1873, it was proclaimed America's largest hotel on any mountain of such height, with 100 sleeping rooms, a 150-seat dining area, and its own orchestra.

Against this backdrop of industrious human enterprise, AMC turned its attention to the more remote northern peaks of the White Mountains. Climbing from a base in Randolph, NH, members explored the massive ridgeline that swept 5 miles southward in a great arc to Mount Washington. This rugged, exposed terrain had only slight dips below 5,000 feet. AMC soon realized that a shelter near treeline would be of great advantage, serving as a convenient base for scientific exploration and providing shelter for hikers crossing the Presidential Range. So, in the summer of 1888, AMC built its first hut, a small stone shelter in the col between Mount Adams and Mount Madison.

Madison Spring Hut was an immediate success. Despite its modest accommodations—simple bunks with pine bough bedding, a few utensils, and a sturdy woodstove—it greatly appealed to men and women of more adventurous spirits. Less spirited were the "cloddish manners" of some visitors who, on more than one occasion, vandalized the hut and ripped up the floor boards or hacked down nearby trees to use for firewood. These early incidents informed AMC's budding approach to conservation and mountain hospitality.

By 1906, AMC had grown exponentially. It had well over a thousand members and was managing multiple shelters and more than 100 miles of trails. It had taken a leadership position in the fight to protect the remnant forests of the White Mountains, much of which were being decimated by indiscriminate logging. Additionally, Madison had undergone an ambitious expansion, and AMC hired its first "care-keeper" to watch over the hut during the summer season. From then on, "hutmasters," as they would come to be known, would occupy each of AMC's huts, and eventually a crew (or "croo," as they prefer to spell it) of "hutmen" would be added to prepare meals and support the growing needs of visitors.

The next few decades would be among AMC's most productive construction periods, with an expanding list of huts at the forefront of AMC's accomplishments. In 1914, AMC built a stone hut in Carter Notch, replacing a log cabin that had been there since 1904. The following summer, at Lakes of the Clouds in the shadow of Mount Washington, AMC built its third hut. By 1920, recognizing a need for a North Country base of operations, AMC built two log cabins on the eastern slope of Mount Washington at Pinkham Notch.

The original Madison Spring Hut (shown here in the 1890s) offered guests blankets, cooking utensils, and other supplies.

In 1922, AMC hired Joseph Brooks Dodge to be the hutmaster at Pinkham Notch. Over the next 37 years, Dodge would have the most profound influence on the high huts of any individual before or since. In his first decade alone, Dodge oversaw the acquisition of Lonesome Lake Hut and the construction of three new huts at Greenleaf, Zealand Falls, and Galehead, establishing a western division of huts that complemented the four huts in the Presidential Range. During this time, he also made improvements to the cabins at Pinkham Notch and enlarged Lakes of the Clouds Hut.

AMC responded to the backpacking boom of the 1960s with construction of a new hut at Mizpah Spring.

Carter Notch Hut's stone building replaced an old log cabin structure in 1914.

Mizpah closed the substantial gap from west to east between the huts at Zealand Falls and Lakes of the Clouds and provided the final link in AMC's chain of high mountain huts. Now, hikers could traverse the high peaks of the White Mountains with comfortable mountain refuges a day's hike apart.

The huts provide visitors much more than hearty meals and a comfortable bunk. They also serve as centers for education, conservation, and mountain leadership. Each hut croo has a resident naturalist who presents educational talks about the surrounding wilderness and AMC's commitment to environmental stewardship. Naturalists encourage participation from youth through the Junior Naturalist program and from all visitors through its Mountain Watch "citizen scientist" initiative, a volunteer-based, long-term study of air quality and forest and alpine plants. At the forefront of AMC's conservation efforts is its Green Promise, a long-standing commitment to sustainable operations and minimizing impact in the backcountry.

Today, AMC's chain of eight high huts is a model for mountain hospitality, stewardship, and backcountry adventure. Since laying its first stone at Madison Spring in 1888, AMC has worked to fulfill its mission of promoting the protection, enjoyment, and understanding of the mountain environment with the same vigor that inspired its founders more than a century ago.

Joe Dodge:
"Father" of the AMC Hut System

Joe Dodge is at the bottom right
of this croo pyramid in 1926.

No one has had a more profound influence on AMC's high huts than Joe Dodge. For 37 years, this legendary huts manager enthusiastically embraced AMC's aspirations and transformed a loosely knit collection of mountain refuges into an exemplary chain of huts devoted to "tramping and mountain hospitality." Above all, through example and a genuine affinity for the people in his employ, Dodge forged a quality of service that continues to inspire the hut system to this day.

Dodge became hutmaster at Pinkham Notch Camp in 1922 and set to work to improve the two seasonal cabins. In 1928, he was named huts manager. By 1932, he had supervised improvements and expansions at existing huts and deftly guided a motley crew of swampers, packers, woodsmen, dynamite specialists, and burros in the construction of three new huts at Greenleaf, Galehead, and Zealand Falls. Somehow, he also managed to co-found the Mount Washington Weather Observatory.

Dodge was a natural leader who expected much from his croos, but never more than he demanded of himself. His indomitable spirit, colorful tongue, and unwavering sense of purpose endeared him to anyone who crossed his path. Indeed, it was once remarked that Dodge "has as many friends as there are trees in New Hampshire."

By 1955, Dodge had become such an institution in New Hampshire that Dartmouth College awarded him an honorary master's degree. Dartmouth called him "…a legend of all that is unafraid, friendly, rigorously good, and ruggedly expressed in the out-of-doors." Dodge retired from AMC in 1959 but continued to promote the understanding and enjoyment of the mountains he loved until his death on October 28, 1973. On that day, a tribute was entered into the Mount Washington Observatory logbook:

> *The Observatory—*
> *The Whole North Country—*
> *Will never be as it was.*
> *Joe Dodge died today.*

2

Geology and Ecology

A MC's high huts provide an excellent opportunity to explore the fascinating natural history of New Hampshire's spectacular White Mountains. From biologically rich wetlands to wind-swept summits, from fir waves to fragile alpine tundra, the region is home to a strikingly diverse and ancient ecosystem.

The White Mountains span a 70-mile segment of the Appalachian Mountain chain and are among the oldest peaks on earth. Indeed, at one time, they were as tall as the Rocky Mountains, but over millions of years, the range has been shaped by an array of natural forces including volcanic disruption, the clash of continents, and the erosive forces of wind, water, and ice. Today, at 6,288 feet, Mount Washington is the region's highest and most prominent summit and the loftiest peak east of the Mississippi River and north of the Carolinas.

AMC Senior Naturalist Nancy Ritger describes the early geology of the White Mountains as "a story of tremendous collisions and ancient continental rifts."

The shallow tarns near Lakes of the Clouds Hut are evidence of the area's glacial past.

Indeed, the exposed terrain seen today among the Presidential and Franconia ranges began to emerge some 400 million years ago, when thick layers of sand and mud at the bottom of a vast inland sea were squeezed between two colliding continents. Under the immense heat and pressure, these layers hardened to form the region's metamorphic rocks, predominantly mica schist, gneiss, and quartzite.

About 200 million years ago, molten rock deep within the earth solidified to form the well-known granite, which today comprises much of the region's bedrock. The bedrock was once more than 7 miles thick, but it was eventually eroded to a nearly flat plain, the remnants of which can be explored near Lakes of the Clouds Hut along the Alpine Garden and Bigelow Lawn. The final lifting of the high peaks occurred during the Cenozoic Era, beginning some 65 million years ago, resulting in a series of sharp peaks formed where the prominent summits of the White Mountains exist today.

It was the tremendous forces of ice and snow during the last Ice Age that ultimately shaped the landscape we are familiar with. Glacial activity scoured ledges, rounded summits, and sculpted the cirques and valleys seen today, including the prominent "notches" at Franconia, Crawford, and Pinkham, and the magnificent amphitheaters of Tuckerman and Huntington ravines. Evidence of glaciation is easily observed near many of the huts in the form of "glacial striae," or debris scratches, left by rocks at the bottom of the receding ice sheet. The scratches generally run in parallel lines in the direction of the ice flow: northwest to southeast.

As the climate warmed and the last of the great ice sheets slowly melted away, the exposed tundra became fertile ground for vegetation. Seeds deposited by birds and animals or blown in by the wind were followed by the emergence of trees some 10,000 years ago. Spruce, pine, birch, and fir advanced northward until only a few square miles of alpine tundra remained, mostly above 4,500 feet along the Presidential Range. Although much diminished, it is the largest contiguous alpine area in the United States east of the Mississippi.

Two major forest types predominate in the White Mountains today: the northern hardwood forest at lower elevations and the boreal forest above 3,000 feet. The northern hardwoods occupy the slopes below 3,000 feet and consist of deciduous hardwoods mixed with red spruce and some balsam fir. The prominent trees include sugar maple (well known for its brilliant fall foliage), American beech, yellow birch, and paper birch. An understory of smaller trees includes stands of striped maple, mountain maple, mountain ash, and pin cherry. White pine forests occur in areas with well-drained sandy soil or on moist, gentle slopes.

The hardy spruce, fir, and balsam conifers of the boreal forest prevail from about 3,000 feet to timberline. Black spruce and balsam fir forests grow at the highest elevations and include the wind-battered, stunted trees known as "krummholz," which can be seen near the highest AMC huts including Greenleaf, Madison Spring, Lakes of the Clouds, and Mizpah Spring. The alpine zone above timberline is reserved for the rare, hearty plants that have adapted to the extremes of weather, including Diapensia, mountain cranberry, alpine azalea, dwarf Lapland rosebay, and Robbins cinquefoil, New England's rarest alpine plant and the focus of a decades-long conservation effort by AMC that led to its down-listing from endangered to threatened. Robbins cinquefoil grows nowhere else on earth.

The name *White Mountains* was likely derived from the prevalence of snow visible atop the high peaks in all seasons. Indeed, the region's unique climatic conditions are among its most remarkable features and greatly affect its ecology. Despite its relatively low elevation, the range lies squarely at the confluence of three major storm tracks. The combination of high winds, severe cold, and frequently wet conditions results in the region's reputation for having some of the world's worst weather.

Mountain Watch

Using an AMC flower guide, hikers gather data to
help track environmental trends.

Visitors to AMC's huts have helped study the effects of
climate change and pollution on the mountain environment since 2005. Mountain Watch, AMC's "citizen
science" program, uses data collected by hikers in a long-term study to assess air quality and plant behavior.

One component of Mountain Watch is the Visibility
Volunteers program. Haze pollution diminishes scenic
views and can negatively affect respiratory and

cardiovascular health. Viz Vols, as the participants are known, track air quality and scenic views by using simple tools such as digital cameras. These observations are combined with weather data and entered into a database that will help researchers understand how haze pollution affects mountain views and the recreational experience.

Another aspect of Mountain Watch is the observation of the flowering and fruit development of alpine and forest plants on mountain trails. Some of the targeted plants include Bigelow's sedge, Diapensia, Labrador tea, and mountain avens, many of which are easily observed near the high huts. The goal of the long-term study is to link flowering time observations to climate data to understand how shifts in climate trends may affect mountain flora. The information gathered also contributes to larger national and regional studies being conducted by the National Phenology Network and the Appalachian Trail Mega-Transect Monitoring Project.

More information about AMC's Mountain Watch program is available at the huts or online at www.outdoors. org/mountainwatch.

3

Planning a Visit

A MC's high huts provide a superb opportunity to enjoy the rugged grandeur of the White Mountains without the encumbrance of a pack laden with heavy camping gear. The promise of a hearty meal and comfortable shelter is a treat after a day on the trail, and the huts are an especially welcome sanctuary after an arduous outing or during inclement weather.

But the expectation of reaching the safety of a mountain shelter should never replace the first rule of the backcountry: BE PREPARED. White Mountain weather is notoriously fickle. Winter-like conditions can occur above treeline in any month of the year, and a great many serious incidents in the mountains occur in spring and fall, when seemingly mild conditions at the trailhead turn potentially life threatening above treeline.

With that in mind, plan your trip with safety as the first objective. Consider the strength of your party and the relative difficulty of the intended route, and above all, anticipate the unexpected. Extra preparation in advance of your excursion can greatly minimize the chances for disaster down the trail. AMC's *White Mountain Guide* is an invaluable resource for trail information and trip planning. You can check current weather and trail conditions by calling the Pinkham Notch Visitor Center at 603-466-2721.

What to Bring

The following list represents the essential gear every mountain traveler should carry regardless of weather or season. It is by no means comprehensive and does not replace good judgment when conditions warrant additional provisions:

Spring/Summer/Fall

Clothing
- ✓ Synthetic or wool base layer (t-shirt, or underwear tops and bottoms)
- ✓ Synthetic or wool long pants (zip-off pants that convert to shorts are popular during warm weather months)
- ✓ Wool sweater or synthetic pile jacket
- ✓ Hat
- ✓ Gloves or mittens
- ✓ Bandanna or handkerchief
- ✓ Wind and rain gear (waterproof/breathable fabrics recommended)
- ✓ Extra socks
- ✓ Sturdy boots

Food and Gear

- ✓ First-aid kit
- ✓ Waterproof matches
- ✓ Knife
- ✓ Whistle
- ✓ Guidebook and trail map
- ✓ Compass
- ✓ High-energy food and snacks
- ✓ Two to four quarts (per person) of water and/or treatment system if near water
- ✓ Flashlight or headlamp with fresh batteries
- ✓ Sunscreen
- ✓ Insect repellent
- ✓ Plastic trash bags (use as pack liners to keep gear dry, for carrying out trash, or as makeshift rain ponchos)
- ✓ Sleeping bag (in case you are forced to sleep out overnight. If traveling in a group, carry at least one sleeping bag. It is an emergency tool that can keep an injured hiker warm until help arrives. Hypothermia is more of a threat when you sit immobilized because of injury.)

IT'S FUN TO

Climb

... when you "travel light"

This is the year to visit
THE WHITE MOUNTAIN
NATIONAL FOREST

Published by the
Appalachian Mountain Club
1940

This AMC brochure was printed in 1940.

Winter

A winter outing to AMC's year-round huts (Lonesome Lake, Zealand Falls, and Carter Notch) can be a thoroughly enjoyable experience. But the demands of winter travel in the backcountry require a comprehensive understanding of conditions and terrain and, in many cases, skills in the use of specialized gear suited for the purpose. For additional information, consult *AMC's Guide to Winter Hiking and Camping*. Or consider one of AMC's many winter skills courses or guided lodge-to-huts outings.

What to Expect
Rooms

- Co-ed bunkrooms, within hut or detached, depending on location. Bunkhouses are not heated, so plan accordingly.
- Separate washrooms with toilets and cold running water (no running water in winter).
- No electrical outlets (energy reserved for emergency communications, kitchen, and lighting of common areas). Bunkrooms have no lighting; bring a headlamp or flashlight.
- Carry in/carry out all trash and recyclables.
- Bunk with pillow and three wool blankets provided during full-service season (bring sheets, sleep sack, or lightweight sleeping bag). Blankets not provided during self-service season (bring an appropriately rated sleeping bag).

Meals

- During full-service season:
  - Dinner and breakfast included with stay.
  - Dinner served family style at 6 P.M. sharp. Includes fresh bread, soup, salad, entrée, and dessert. Child-friendly meal options available at all huts. With advanced notice, the huts can accommodate dietary preferences including vegetarian, vegan, gluten-free, and lactose-free diets.
  - Breakfast served family style at 7 A.M. sharp. Includes eggs or pancakes, plus hot cereal, fruit, breakfast meat like bacon or sausage, and coffee or tea.
  - Lunch—bring your own; otherwise soup and baked goods available for purchase during the day.
- During self-service season:
  - Guests pack in own food and have full use of hut's stove, oven, cookware, and service ware.
  - Caretaker available 7–10 A.M. and 4–10 P.M.; caretaker may light fire in woodstove on winter evenings.

Base Camps

AMC's Joe Dodge Lodge/Pinkham Notch Visitor Center and the Highland Center at Crawford Notch provide ideal starting points to visit the high huts. Both locations offer a broad range of programs, information, and essential gear to help you prepare for venturing into the backcountry, and both provide ample accommodations to begin or end your trip to the White Mountains. They are also stops on AMC's Hiker Shuttle, which serves major trailheads to all eight huts.

Pinkham Notch has served as AMC's North Country base of operations since 1920 and is a popular hub for exploring the Presidential Range in all seasons. Joe Dodge Lodge offers a variety of bunk and family rooms, with meals offered at the nearby Visitor Center. For reservations, call 603-466-2727 or visit www.outdoors.org/lodging. The Visitor Center front desk is available 24 hours a day at 603-466-2721.

The Highland Center is located at the height of land at Crawford Notch between Zealand Falls Hut to the west and Mizpah Spring Hut north and east. It offers bunkrooms and private rooms in the lodge, as well as lower-cost shared bunk space in the Shapleigh Bunkhouse. For reservations, call 603-466-2727 or visit www.outdoors.org/lodging. To reach the front desk (24 hours), call 603-278-HIKE.

AMC's Hiker Shuttle

Anyone planning a hut-to-hut excursion should consider using AMC's convenient Hiker Shuttle. The shuttle offers transportation from Joe Dodge Lodge/Pinkham Notch Visitor Center and the Highland Center to all major approach routes to the huts. The shuttle operates daily from early June through mid-September, and on weekends and holidays through mid-October. Reservations are required—call 603-466-2727. For more information, visit AMC's website at www.outdoors.org/whitemountains.

"Da Croo"

Croo members carry an injured thru-hiker
3.9 miles down the steep Valley Way Trail.

Nothing exemplifies the character of AMC's hut system more than the young men and women who come to the mountains to work in the high huts. Tasked with packing in supplies and passing along respect for and understanding of the natural world, among many other responsibilities, hut crews must be multitalented and energetic. They are at once cooks, caretakers, educators, search-and-rescue workers, and entertainers.

In the early days, teams of two to four "hutmen" were enlisted from New England colleges (particularly Dartmouth) to pack in provisions, watch over the huts, and provide guests with fresh blankets and warm meals. A fraternal spirit grew naturally among "Da Croo" (as they began calling themselves), and they often challenged one another to see who could carry the heaviest loads. Friendly rivalries between the huts evolved into so-called "raids," with croos from one hut setting out (usually at night) to invade another hut and search for prized possessions (signs, an airplane propeller, even a canoe!).

Fun and fortitude aside, the croos adhered to a strict code of conduct outlined by Huts Manager Joe Dodge in *The Hutman's Handbook, Season of 1935,* still considered an essential guide. Dodge insisted they exemplify qualities of "verve, vigor, alacrity, and perspicacity," tall tasks for young men barely out of their teens.

Women were initially excluded from working at the huts, but during World War II, married couples often became caretakers because of the absence of available manpower. The first "unofficial" female croo members were called "Hutmen F." Evolving cultural mores during the 1960s eventually demanded AMC relax its concerns regarding male/female crew cohabitation. By the 1970s, women were serving alongside men at the huts, and today they often comprise more than half of the croo.

Working at the huts requires a combination of guest service skills and backcountry experience. On any given day, a croo member might deliver a playful "BFD" (blanket folding demonstration) or assist in a search-and-rescue operation. Sixteen of the 49 croo positions are reserved for the roles of hutmasters and assistant hutmasters. One croo member at each hut is also chosen to be the season's hut naturalist.

4
Lonesome Lake Hut

First opened: 1930

Elevation: 2,760 feet

Coordinates: 44° 08′ 18″ N, 71° 42′ 12″ W

Location: Franconia Notch State Park, near Cannon
Mountain

Sleeping capacity: 48 in 2 detached bunkhouses

Seasons: year-round (full service in summer, self service in
fall, winter, and spring)

Green systems in use: solar panels, solar water preheat,
composting toilets, food composting, and compact fluorescent
lighting

Interesting Fact: first all-female hut croo (1979)

About the Hut

Lonesome Lake is an ideal destination for novice hikers, families, or first-time visitors to AMC's chain of huts. The relatively modest ascent to the hut affords an excellent introduction to the challenges of mountain exploration and its abundant rewards. Here you'll find a biologically diverse wilderness, superb panoramic views, and an enticing glacial tarn to splash away the sweat and toil of a day on the trail. For more experienced outdoor enthusiasts, the hut also serves as a convenient base camp for year-round adventures.

Lonesome is the westernmost hut on the Appalachian Trail (AT). It is situated at the southern flank of Cannon Mountain with a spectacular northeastern vista across the lake to the high peaks along Franconia Ridge. For thru-hikers, the hut provides a brief refuge before tackling the celebrated and demanding mountains yet to come. For shorter outings, it's an idyllic setting to explore the White Mountains environment.

The hut's main building, sometimes referred to as "the round house" by the croo, is an octagonal structure, vaguely reminiscent of a yurt. It and two adjacent bunkhouses were originally constructed in 1964. AMC has been established here since 1930, and the first structures built at the lake date back to the nineteenth century. In 1876, W. C. (William Cowper) Prime, a noted journalist, art historian, and travel writer, built adjacent cabins at the northeastern edge of the lake to serve as a

Guests enjoy fine views from the dock at Lonesome Lake.

fishing camp. Prime was an early advocate for the preservation of the "primeval forest," and he felt an intimate connection to the area:

There are hundreds of birch trees on the mountain-side, and on the ridge, and around the lake, each of which I know, and of these there are perhaps twenty or thirty with which I have had long relations of friendship. I would not have the woodsman's axe touch any tree on this mountain for any money. Every one is a friend.

In 1923, a devastating fire swept through Franconia Notch, leveling the famous grand hotel near Echo Lake known as the Profile House. The owners chose not to rebuild, and as a result, speculators quickly moved in to evaluate the value of the region's timber. This fostered a campaign, spearheaded by the Society for the Protection of New Hampshire Forests, to purchase and preserve the area. In 1928, those efforts culminated in the establishment of the Franconia Notch Forest Reservation and War Memorial, known today as Franconia Notch State Park. The following year, the state of New Hampshire acquired Lonesome Lake, Prime's cabins, and the land surrounding them to incorporate into the park. Soon after, the state leased the cabins to AMC.

AMC welcomed the addition to its growing list of backcountry huts (Greenleaf was planned and built that very year). It renovated the cabins, added a kitchen and dining area, and opened the doors to visitors during the summer of 1930. With the exception of badly needed repairs to the women's bunkhouse in 1950, the cabin and adjoining facilities remained in use until the early 1960s. In 1964, the near-century-old cabins were removed, and the New Hampshire Division of Parks built the new hut and bunkhouses on the southern end of the lake, which opened under AMC management in its continuing partnership with the state. In 2008, AMC's Construction Crew gave Lonesome Lake Hut a major update. New doors, larger windows, a metal roof, pine paneling, and exterior cedar shingles were all added to enhance efficiency and aesthetics.

Today, the hut receives a steady stream of visitors and is especially popular with families eager to introduce their children to the backcountry experience. To that end, AMC has developed several programs at Lonesome specifically geared for kids. Trekkers and snowshoers are also drawn to Lonesome's quiet beauty in winter. Since 2002, the hut has been open to visitors in winter on a self-service basis. During the cold season, the caretaker lights the main building's woodstove at 4 P.M.

Natural History

The Lonesome Lake habitat is the most biologically rich and diverse ecosystem at the doorstep of any of the high huts. From moss to moose, bogs to balsams, snowshoe hares to sundews, opportunities abound for observing a unique and interesting display of flora and fauna.

The lake itself is a classic glacial tarn, the remnant of a massive ice sheet that scoured the region thousands of years ago, scooping out small depressions in the granite where shallow pools of water formed following its retreat. Although the lake encompasses little more than 12 acres, with an average depth of only 3 to 6 feet, it feeds important watersheds that reach all the way to the Atlantic Ocean. From its outlet at Cascade Brook, Lonesome's cool water flows southward over ledges and waterfalls until it joins other streams that give rise to the Pemigewasset River. The "Pemi," in turn, continues southward until it meets the mighty Merrimack River along its journey to the sea in Newburyport, Mass.

Lonesome Lake sits on acidic rock and is largely bounded by similarly acidic bog vegetation. Yet it supports a healthy population of brook trout and an array of other plants and animals. The key to this life-giving water is the feldspar found high above on Kinsman Ridge. As weathered feldspar crystals erode and flow into Lonesome, they leach soluble calcium, which buffers and neutralizes much of the acidity seeping from the Conway granite beneath and around the lake.

The boggy areas around Lonesome are well worth exploration and are easily accessible via connective trails encircling the lake. Raised planks and footbridges have been placed along the path to protect the fragile terrain and afford an excellent opportunity to view the boggy areas up close. The thick mats of sphagnum moss (also known as peat moss) found here retain tremendous amounts of water, up to 20 times their dry weight, but are highly acidic and nutrient poor. As a result, this important wetland ecosystem supports a variety of flora and fauna specially adapted to the challenging conditions. Carnivorous plants, such as the beautiful sundew, are a prime example. Without sufficient nutrients to draw from the soil, the sundew attracts and traps unsuspecting insects by emitting a sweet, sticky drop of liquid at the end of its many tentacle-like glands. Once captured, the insect is slowly digested and its vital nutrients extracted.

Excursions

There are several interesting and worthwhile trips within a day's outing from Lonesome Lake Hut. Nature lovers and families will enjoy the casual loop around the tarn. Intrepid hikers may prefer the 6.5-mile loop to Kinsman Pond via Kinsman Ridge and the Cannon Balls and back. For peak baggers aspiring to the 4,000 Footer Club, Cannon Mountain (4,100 feet), North Kinsman (4,293 feet), and South Kinsman (4,358 feet) are all worthy, attainable climbs from the hut. For detailed information, consult AMC's *White Mountain Guide*.

Access to the Hut

Difficulty: easy
Distance: 1.6 miles
Hiking time: 1 hour, 15 minutes

AMC's Lonesome Lake Trail (in conjunction with small sections of Cascade Brook Trail and Fishin' Jimmy Trail) is by far the most popular route to the hut. The path begins from Lafayette Campground near a footbridge that crosses over the Pemigewasset River, and ascends 950 feet in elevation. The hut can also be reached from Cascade Brook Trail (via Whitehouse Trail or Basin-Cascades Trail) from the Franconia Notch Parkway, by Fishin' Jimmy Trail from Kinsman Junction, or by Dodge Cutoff from Hi-Cannon Trail.

Junior
Naturalist

Young hikers take the Junior Naturalist pledge,
promising to respect the birds, bees,
flowers, and trees.

With a full-time naturalist at each hut, AMC's high hut visitors have the opportunity gain a deeper understanding of their mountain surroundings. Young hikers are encouraged to participate in the Junior Naturalist program. It's an exciting, hands-on, environmental awareness program designed to help kids learn about the natural world and their important role in helping to protect it.

Using the Junior Naturalist Activity Book, young people can complete exercises on natural history, safety in the outdoors, minimum impact hiking, and natural resource protection. There are three activity books available: one for ages 5–8, one for ages 9–12, and one of winter activities. Through multiple-choice questions, crossword puzzles, and open-ended queries, kids practice Leave No Trace ethics, learn how to read contour lines on a map, test their wilderness skills, observe the weather on their hike, and much more. The activity books introduce children to the unique elements of the White Mountain ecosystem and navigate them toward a greater appreciation of the natural environment.

Once children complete their activity book, they receive a colorful patch and a Junior Naturalist certificate in an impromptu graduation ceremony conducted by members of the hut croo. Approximately 2,500 kids participate in the Junior Naturalist program at AMC's White Mountain locations each year.

The skills Junior Naturalists learn while staying at the huts can easily be applied to their home lives as well. Junior Naturalists walk away with more respect for the natural world and an understanding of their role in protecting our planet—whether they're on vacation, hiking in the mountains, or playing in their backyard.

5

Greenleaf Hut

First opened: 1930

Elevation: 4,220 feet

Coordinates: 44° 09′ 37″ N, 71° 39′ 37″ W

Location: Mount Lafayette, Franconia Ridge

Sleeping capacity: 48 in 3 partitioned bunkrooms (for 6 or more)

Season: early May to mid-October (caretaker basis in May)

Green systems in use: solar panels, wind generator, waterless toilets, food composting, and compact fluorescent lighting

Interesting fact: first hut to have running water and indoor toilets

About the Hut

In 1929, when the state of New Hampshire asked AMC to operate its recently acquired cabins at Lonesome Lake as part of the hut system, AMC readily agreed, but there was a problem. AMC's North Country base of operations at Pinkham Notch and the established huts at Lakes, Madison, and Carter were roughly 50 miles east. Huts Manager Joe Dodge later recalled, "...running 'em kind of all separate from everything else didn't make much sense."

Dodge met with AMC's Hut Committee to figure out the logistics of managing Lonesome. Those meetings led to a more ambitious plan to establish a "western division" of huts. As luck would have it, a benefactor had recently given money to AMC to build a mountain shelter for hikers. Colonel Charles Greenleaf was the proprietor of the Profile House in Franconia Notch, one of the lavish grand hotels of the era. His generosity would help AMC establish its first newly constructed hut west of the Presidential Range.

Dodge had a perfect spot in mind. In the summer of 1929, construction crews, aided for the first time by donkeys, began hauling materials and supplies to an impossibly beautiful plein air plateau on the shoulder of Mount Lafayette. Under Dodge's supervision, a new hut, unlike any AMC had built before, was swiftly completed and ready to receive guests in the summer of 1930. In honor of the Colonel's generous bequest, the new facility was named Greenleaf. "Now," Dodge would later pronounce, "the Colonel has his hut...where you

A croo member prepares the salad course for a full crowd of hungry hikers at Greenleaf Hut.

can look across at the same mountains he would see from his hotel."

Greenleaf Hut represented a substantial change in hut design. For one thing, the structure was built mostly of wood, with the exception of the south-facing dining room wall of stone. The stone huts at Lakes and Madison were certainly sturdy, but they also tended to be damp and cold. Greenleaf's interior was designed with comfort and convenience in mind. A central kitchen and common room/dining area were flanked by bunkrooms on either side. Greenleaf was also the first hut to have running water and inside toilets, substantial conveniences in the high country. In 1989, the kitchen and common room/dining area were expanded to enhance comfort and capacity.

As Greenleaf approaches a century of service, it continues to be one of AMC's most visited huts and the flagship of the Western Division. On any given day in summer, a steady stream of hikers can be found stopping at the hut or taking a break from the trail to enjoy the magnificent views from its deck or doorstep.

Natural History

Greenleaf Hut lies near the eastern lip of Franconia Notch, an awe-inspiring example of the collaborative forces of wind, water, ice, and time. At an elevation of 4,220 feet, the hut is situated squarely in the alpine transition zone (known as the ecotone), where trees quickly yield to tundra. Here, even the casual observer will appreciate nature's

Nightly talks are part of AMC's high hut experience. Here, Greenleaf's hutmaster discusses the history of packboards.

dramatic interplay. No other hut in the system has such a variety of ecosystems at its doorstep.

The notch is bounded by the Franconia Range on the east and the Kinsman Range and Cannon Mountain to the west. The deep, U-shaped notch seen today was originally cut in a V shape by the erosive forces of water. At the end of the Pleistocene epoch, ice moved in and scoured the walls and valley below. With its sheer granite walls, Cannon Cliff is now a favorite destination for adventurous rock and ice climbers.

Below the hut, the forest is relatively protected, buffered along a receding slope line; the trees stand tall, reaching skyward for precious sunlight. But as you emerge onto Lafayette's shoulder, into the open air, the trees begin to crumple and wilt from bitter, unimpeded winds churning through Franconia Notch. The effect is striking. The dwarfed trees that survive huddle to the ground in what is known as a "krummholz formation." Krummholz is a German word that roughly translates as "crooked" or "twisted" wood.

As you climb higher, the trees surrender entirely to tundra. There are three types of tundra worldwide: arctic, antarctic, and alpine. All types are characterized by the commonalities of low temperatures and a short growing season. Alpine tundra occurs only at high altitudes and lacks the characteristic permafrost (permanently frozen soil) that denotes arctic environments and the vast ice fields common to the antarctic ecozone.

Alpine soils generally drain well and support an array of dwarf shrubs and plants that are well adapted to survive nature's sometimes harsh hand but are no match for a hiker's crushing footfalls. Anyone venturing onto Franconia Ridge will notice the low rock walls on either side of the trail. When these "alpine scree walls" were first introduced by AMC in 1977, they received a mixed reaction from the hiking community because of their "unnatural appearance." But the technique quickly proved its merits by encouraging hikers to stay on the trail and allowing the fragile alpine plants an opportunity to rejuvenate.

Greenleaf Hut overlooks a picturesque, shallow tarn known as Eagle Lake. The lake lies in a depression beneath Lafayette's summit and is an excellent example of ecological succession. The bog vegetation is moving in along the lake's shorelines. Over time (perhaps a few thousand years), the bog vegetation will soak up all the water and transform Eagle Lake into a terrestrial, sediment-laden basin of plants and peat moss. For now, there is ample water to support an array of aquatic plants and animals from pond lilies to peepers.

Excursions

The obvious outing from Greenleaf Hut is an ascent of Mount Lafayette and a traverse of Franconia Ridge. In good weather, this should not be missed. The climb is enjoyable, and the views from the top are magnificent.

There are interesting, much less demanding walks nearby too. The North Outlook (commonly referred to as Sunset Rocks) from Greenleaf Trail is a short stroll from the hut. It's a perfect destination to soak up a sunset and take in the brilliant panorama overlooking the cliffs of Cannon Mountain and Franconia Notch. This, incidentally, is the only place in the chain where two huts can be viewed by one another (Greenleaf to Lonesome Lake and vice versa).

At 5,260 feet, Mount Lafayette is the highest mountain in the Franconia Range. There are stunning views of the Pemigewasset Wilderness Area from Lafayette's summit. The range itself is second only to the Presidentials in elevation in the White Mountains, but their respective ridgelines contrast markedly. The Presidential Range is generally broad and massive, while the Franconia Range is narrow, sharp, and serrated. Franconia's high peaks appear distinct and imposing. AMC's *White Mountain Guide* aptly describes them as suggestive of a "gigantic medieval cathedral...like towers supported by soaring buttresses that rise from the floor of the notch."

From Greenleaf Hut, Lafayette rises just over 1,000 feet in 1.1 miles along Greenleaf Trail. Allow 1 hour for the ascent and 30 minutes for the return. At the summit, pick up Franconia Ridge Trail for the traverse (1.7 miles one way). For good reason, this is one of the most popular hikes in the White Mountains and is usually coupled with scenic Falling Waters Trail at the foot of Little Haystack Mountain to form a long loop hike connecting with Old Bridle Path. (Please note, the ridge and high peaks are extremely exposed and should not be attempted in bad weather. Consult AMC's *White Mountain Guide* for details and descriptions.)

Access to the Hut

Difficulty: moderate
Distance: 2.7 or 2.9 miles
Hiking time: 2.5 hours

Two trails lead directly to Greenleaf Hut from the Franconia Notch Parkway: Greenleaf Trail from Cannon Mountain Tramway parking lot, and Old Bridle Path from Lafayette Place parking lot (accessible from both sides of the Parkway).

Greenleaf is the shorter (2.7 miles) and less traveled of the two. Though it has few wide, sweeping views, the moss-covered rocks and trees draped with lichen make it a beautiful journey.

Old Bridle Path is heavily used, but for good reason. It affords excellent views from several open ledges and ascends in (mostly) moderate fashion, gaining 2,450 feet over 2.9 miles.

Allow a minimum of 2.5 hours for either trail. Pay particular attention to weather conditions in the area, as Franconia Ridge is susceptible to high winds and bad weather.

Packboards

**This croo member is carrying
supplies to Mizpah Spring Hut.**

Since the 1930s, AMC's hut croos have been carrying supplies to the high huts using a simple wood, canvas, and leather contraption called a packboard. Indeed, today's packboards are almost identical to the ones described nearly 80 years ago:

The packframe is nothing but a wooden corset for the back, all set about with hooks. It accommodates itself nicely to the carrying of boxes, stoves, kerosene tins, and wheel-barrows. To fit a load onto it, you heap the boxes or what you will on its back and lash them securely with a rope to the many hooks.

The croo's preference for packboards has as much to do with practical application as it does with tradition. Try strapping a wheelbarrow to a modern internal frame backpack or loading it with fifteen dozen eggs! Despite their seemingly antiquated design, packboards have proven invaluable for transporting the typically heavy, sometimes awkward loads of fresh food and supplies the croos must carry to the huts twice each week.

In the early years, a spirited competition quickly grew among hutmen as to who could pack in the heaviest loads. At the time, loads weighing 200 pounds or more were common. But in 1938, a group of AMC members presented a petition to the club president "concerning the effect of backpacking upon the hutmen stationed at the various Club huts," specifically upon their hearts. The hut committee surveyed 109 former hutmen to determine whether they showed "effects of excessive exertion." Finding none, the committee nevertheless decreed that all hutmen should cease "stunt" packing and have physicals before and after every season.

Today, packing is more often a collaborative affair, and hut croos share their burdens equally. Nonetheless, loads still average a very respectable 40 to 80 pounds.

First opened: 1932

Elevation: 3,780 feet

Coordinates: 44° 11′ 16″ N, 71° 34′ 08″ W

Location: Garfield Ridge, Pemigewasset Wilderness

Sleeping capacity: 38 in 4 co-ed bunkrooms

Season: early May to mid-October (caretaker basis in May)

Green systems in use: solar panels, wind generation, waterless toilets, food composting, and compact fluorescent lighting

Interesting fact: built to withstand gale-force winds

About the Hut

Secluded Galehead, AMC's most remote hut, is perched on a small rise overlooking the vast Pemigewasset Wilderness, New Hampshire's largest and most storied tract of federally protected backcountry terrain. At nearly 5 miles from the closest trailhead and more than 7 miles from the nearest hut, Galehead is a welcomed sanctuary for many mountain travelers. It's also an excellent base camp to explore the heart of the White Mountain National Forest.

The original hut at Galehead was built in 1931, during a whirlwind of expansion that included the construction of Zealand Falls Hut in the same year and Greenleaf Hut two years prior. Collectively, the three huts bridged the substantial gap between AMC's westernmost facility at Lonesome Lake and the long-established huts in the Presidential Range. Both Galehead and Zealand Falls were modeled after Greenleaf in design, with a central kitchen and common area flanked by two wings to accommodate men's and women's bunks.

The plan for Galehead also included building the hut from native timbers, and according to Huts Manager Joe Dodge, it was a "rough, pioneering job." "Swampers" and "graders" set to work in early July to establish a pack trail sufficiently passable to haul in materials using pack mules, or "donks," as Dodge called them. Meanwhile, the wood crew set up camp at Galehead shelter, which was next to the planned hut site. Working rain or shine, they began "cutting logs within a hundred yards of the site,

A wind generator atop Galehead Hut harnesses energy for indoor lighting.

which were then twitched in by a team of horses, peeled and yarded."

By October 5, the exterior of the hut was complete, but materials for the hut's interior still needed to be packed in. As Dodge recalled it, "the packers were having dire trouble driving the donks up the muddy trail." The combination of rain and hooves had churned the path to nearly impassable muck. Fortunately, late in the season they got a break in the weather and were able to deliver the remaining goods. In all, the packers and donks hauled in nearly 32 tons of materials to the Galehead site.

However challenging Galehead's construction may have been, the crew built a sturdy structure. On September 21, 1938, just six years after the hut was completed, a ferocious, record-setting hurricane slammed New England. That day, the Mount Washington Observatory clocked sustained winds of 136 MPH. The devastation was extensive: 57,000 homes were damaged or destroyed, and nearly 800 people lost their lives. The storm leveled most of the trees surrounding Galehead and along the ridgelines nearby, but the hut survived intact.

Ultimately, it was the ravages of time that compromised Galehead. After 60 years of service, the hut was in dire need of updating. AMC considered a major renovation, but that would have required replacing most of the building, without benefit of redesign to meet modern needs and standards. Instead, in 1999, AMC opted to completely rebuild the hut.

The new facility opened to the public in June 2000, blending the best of the original building's heritage with modern innovations, including smaller bunkrooms, alternative energy systems, and composting toilets. The sturdy, aesthetically pleasing structure was built to withstand winds of 125 MPH and ground snow loading of 100 pounds per square foot. Galehead was also AMC's first backcountry hut designed to meet federal Americans with Disabilities Act (ADA) requirements. On August 15, 2000, a determined group of hikers with disabilities (3 in wheelchairs, and 2 on crutches) supported by friends, family, and volunteers completed the rugged ascent to Galehead in 12 hours.

Natural History

The magnificent views of seemingly unbroken, undulating green forest enjoyed from Galehead Hut today belie the region's historical reality. Prior to 1880, the "great wilderness" simply known then as "Pemigewasset" was a seldom visited, untracked, primeval forest. Indeed, Moses Sweetser's *The White Mountains: A Handbook for Travelers*, first published in 1876, cautioned "…this inner solitude should be entered only under the guidance of experienced foresters and traveling will be found very slow and arduous." But even when Sweetser's description of the "Pemi" was written, the region was already being subjected to radical change.

Between 1880 and 1940, the region was quite literally laid waste by logging. The arrival of the railroad allowed timber speculators access to great stands of virgin forest in the White Mountains as never before. At the height of the industry, the Pemigewasset contained the largest railroad system in the White Mountains, including an amazing 72 rail lines. In all, more than one billion board feet of timber were removed from the 66,000-acre watershed. Much of the wood was used to produce clothespins, heel stock for shoes, wooden flooring, and paper plates.

Between unsustainable clear cutting, unchecked fires that swept through and devoured the remaining slash, and the Great Hurricane of 1938, the Pemigewasset region had been pretty well battered by the time the U.S. Forest Service stepped in to acquire the watershed in 1946. But the resilience of nature is quite remarkable, and a slow process of regeneration soon began. By 1984, the region had recovered sufficiently to warrant its designation as an official Wilderness Area. Today, the Pemigewasset Wilderness includes 45,000 acres of beautiful backcountry terrain with nearly 60 miles of maintained hiking and backpacking trails to explore.

Scanning across the Pemigewasset's ridges and valleys, Galehead visitors will likely notice gray, linear or crescent-shaped bands of dead trees in the otherwise healthy forest. These are particularly evident along the Twin Range. They are known as "fir waves" and are a natural occurrence common to high-elevation fir forests in the White Mountians, the Adirondacks, and Japan.

Fir waves form when natural gaps in the forest canopy are exposed to stress from wind and weather. At the same time, young trees begin to grow in the

Visitors enjoy a hearty breakfast at Galehead's long wooden tables.

windward, protected area of the gap and eventually form a line of healthy, green forest. The combination of dying trees at the leeward edge and regenerating trees at the windward edge results in the spread of fir waves in the direction of the prevailing wind. Wave regeneration is estimated to occur in 60-year intervals.

Excursions

Galehead Hut provides a convenient base camp from which to explore the Pemigewasset Wilderness. There are also several interesting day outings, including a short, steep ascent of South Twin Mountain, at 4,902 feet, New Hampshire's eighth highest peak, or a long jaunt to the pools and cascades known as 13 Falls.

To scale South Twin Mountain, pick up Twinway Trail from the hut. The path passes over a ledge with an outlook, descends briefly, and then begins to climb steeply to the summit cone. The distance is only 0.8 mile, but you'll climb 1,150 feet to reach the bare summit, so allow at least 1 hour for the ascent.

Frost Trail leads from Galehead Hut to the summit of Galehead Mountain. Leaving the hut, it descends, then makes a sharp right at a junction where Twin Brook Trail enters left. After a short distance, Frost Trail ascends a steep pitch. At the top, a side path leads left to an excellent view over the Twin Brook valley. The distance is 0.5 mile. Allow half an hour for the round-trip excursion.

13 Falls is located deep in the heart of the Pemigewasset Wilderness. The remote waterfalls range in height from about 5 feet to 25 feet and include several cold-water pools to enjoy on a hot summer day. They are located near the 13 Falls Tent Site, at the junction of Franconia Brook and Twin Brook Trails, approximately 2.7 miles from Galehead Hut. Consult AMC's *White Mountain Guide* for specific trail descriptions, and allow at least 4 hours for the round-trip journey.

Access to the Hut

Difficulty: moderate
Distance: 4.6 miles
Hiking time: 3.5 hours

Direct access to Galehead Hut is via Gale River Trail. The trailhead is reached from Gale River Loop Road (FR 25 and FR 92), which is located off Route 3 approximately 5 miles south of the village of Twin Mountain.

The 4.2-mile path ascends steadily, with a steeper grade near its junction with Garfield Ridge Trail. (The trail lies within the watershed of a municipal water supply, and hikers should take care not to pollute any of the streams in this watershed.) From there, it's another 0.4 mile of climbing to the hut. Allow 3.5 hours.

The Donks

"Mule skinners" guided teams of donkeys
loaded with building materials and supplies to the huts.

AMC's archives are filled with tall tales of sturdy men shouldering impossibly heavy loads to supply the huts with essential goods and materials—men like Bud Hefti, who reputedly hauled 224 pounds to Madison Spring Hut in 1940, or Sid Havely, who is said to have shouldered 331 pounds of plumbing equipment to Lakes of the Clouds Hut in 1969. But a herd of lesser known packers rightfully earned their place in the record books too.

Old Jack, Whitey, Trigger, Little Hoss, and Smokey were just a few of the stubborn but reliable burros that carried supplies to AMC's high huts for more than three decades. The notion of using donkeys to ferry provisions to the huts originated in 1929 when two former hutmen established the White Mountain Jackass Company and proposed their packing services to AMC. Their timing was perfect. AMC was about to embark on a massive expansion that would include renovations to existing huts and, soon after, construction of three new huts.

Huts Manager Joe Dodge agreed to try the "donks," as he called them, so 41 burros were delivered from Roswell, N.M., to Randolph, N.H. The burros were not as keen to participate in the fledgling enterprise, and soon there was "trouble aplenty," as Dodge recalled it. "The boys had an idea that these donkeys could be loaded up and driven up the mountain without much effort, but they were certainly disillusioned."

To remedy the situation, Dodge hired an experienced mule skinner to drive the mules. In short order, the donks fell in line and more than proved their value. In that first year alone, man and beast shared the burden of delivering 60 tons of equipment to support a renovation at Madison Spring Hut and the construction of Greenleaf Hut.

After just one season, the owners of the White Mountain Jackass Company decided to pursue other interests. Recognizing the donks' usefulness, AMC assumed ownership of the herd. For the next 35 years, burros hauled materials and equipment to the huts each spring. They were also the main attraction of Gorham, N.H.'s annual 4th of July parade. In 1964, transport helicopters began delivering payloads to the huts, and the donks were let out to pasture for good.

7

Zealand Falls Hut

Visitor Stamp

First opened: 1932

Elevation: 2,640 feet

Coordinates: 44° 11′ 44″ N, 71° 29′ 39″ W

Location: Zealand Valley, White Mountain National Forest

Sleeping capacity: 36 in 2 co-ed bunkrooms

Season: year-round (full service in summer and early fall, self service in late fall, winter, and spring)

Green systems in use: solar panels, wind generation, hydropower, composting toilets, food composting, and compact fluorescent lighting

Interesting fact: the only hut with hydropower

About the Hut

AMC's hut at Zealand Falls is the quintessential cabin in the woods. Its inviting front porch, cozy dining area, and comfy bunkrooms evoke the charming, casual demeanor of a traditional New England camp. Despite the hut's relatively low altitude (2,640 feet), it has magnificent views and is situated just steps away from a lovely waterfall that cascades over open ledges to Zealand Pond, 200 feet below. In all seasons, it's an accessible, relaxing backcountry retreat.

Built in 1931, Zealand (along with Greenleaf and Galehead) completed AMC's goal of creating a hut-to-hut system that allowed hikers to reach the next shelter in a day's walk. Zealand also effectively closed the gap between the Western Division huts and those in the Presidential Range. Although construction of the hut was completed in just three months, it was an arduous task that required persistence and a good measure of pluck.

AMC Huts Manager Joe Dodge had the hut pre-cut, framed, and marked at a Vermont mill-yard to reduce the amount of materials necessary to pack in to the site. Burros were used to carry the heavy loads, but Dodge also employed an old Fordson tractor that he christened the "Zealand Hot Shot." The tractor "stood the gaff," Dodge recalled, but the long journey to the hut site was not without incident.

In the midst of an unrelenting rain, the tractor threw a bearing that required a "complete disemboweling of the heavy machine three miles up the trail." After three days' work, the tractor was repaired, but the ignition system

The beautiful chutes and pools of Whitewall Brook at Zealand Falls Hut provide a wonderful place to dip your feet after a day on the trail.

was rain-soaked, and a fire had to be built to dry it out. By then, high water and mud had made the route all but impassable, and three donkeys were nearly lost at a dam crossing. Nevertheless, the combination of burros and tractor ultimately proved to be much more economical than sheer manpower.

Situating the hut in the Zealand Valley represented a symbolic victory for AMC's commitment to conservation. Only a few decades earlier, the valley's forests had been so decimated by indiscriminate logging that one chronicler compared it to Dante's entrance to Hell: "All hope abandon ye who enter here." But AMC's persistent lobbying was instrumental in saving the region from further unchecked deforestation and, eventually, led the way to establishing the White Mountain National Forest.

By 1876, the year AMC was founded, more than half of New Hampshire's forests had been cleared, and the state had sold off the last of its North Country holdings (including the summit of Mount Washington) to private interests. The arrival of the railroad had also opened the door to large-scale timber operations in the once impenetrable mountains. About the same time, controversial lumber baron J.E. Henry was acquiring several tracts of virgin timberlands in the Zealand River Valley.

By 1880, Henry had established the village of "Zealand" along the banks of the Ammonoosuc River (near the site of today's campground), complete with sawmill, housing for 300 employees, post office, coal kilns, and a company store, and constructed a standard-gauge logging railroad alongside the Zealand River. At least six logging camps were constructed in deeper parts of the valley where the railroad could not reach. Well-paid workmen spent 11-hour days hauling out coveted spruce timber.

Clear-cut logging in the valley continued unabated until 1886, when sparks from one of Henry's railroad engines ignited a forest fire that burned for a week and destroyed nearly 12,000 acres, much of it virgin spruce. The fire also ignited a public outcry and sparked a movement to safeguard the natural resources of the White Mountains.

AMC, along with the Society for the Protection of New Hampshire Forests and the New Hampshire Forestry Commission, tirelessly pursued a resolution to end the "unwise and barbarous" logging practices. In time, they developed the concept of a government-owned "forest reservation" that would be managed for multiple purposes, including recreation and sustainable forestry. After years of debate, in 1911, Congress finally passed the Appalachian–White Mountains Forest Reservation Bill (commonly known as the Weeks Act), which established the eastern National Forest system and led to the creation of the White Mountain National Forest.

Natural History

The Zealand Valley is a testament to nature's resilience. Little more than a century has passed since it was literally stripped bare, burned over, and left for dead. Yet today the valley once again hosts a thriving, complex forest. Nowhere else in New England is there a better example of post-fire succession and regeneration after such devastation. From the ashes grew ground shrubs and pin cherry. Larger hardwoods followed, including birch, maple, and beech. In time, red spruce and balsam fir will once again dominate, and the forest will look much as it did before.

In recent years, another eager "timber baron" has moved into Zealand: Castor Canadensis, also known as the North American beaver. Evidence of its handiwork is readily observed at Zealand Pond and along Zealand Trail north of the hut. While this industrious rodent may, on occasion, disrupt the work of trail crews, it is a welcome addition to the valley.

Beavers were revered by American Indians as the "sacred center of the land." They were a valued source of meat, skins, and medicine. European settlers in New England also valued their pelts and oil. In Connecticut and Massachusetts alone, more than 10,000 beavers per year were trapped for the fur trade between 1620 and 1630. By the late 1800s, they had been trapped to extinction in southern New England and very nearly so in New Hampshire. Six breeding pairs were released into the state between 1926 and 1930 as part of a restocking program. By 1955, the entire state was repopulated, and they are once again thriving throughout New England.

Beavers build their dams in shallow valleys, altering the flow of rivers and streams, which subsequently creates a rich wetland habitat for an array of animals including fish, frogs, birds, turtles, and moose. They are

Members of Zealand's croo enjoy some downtime before dinner duties.

North America's largest rodent, ranging in weight from 30 to 100 pounds. The beaver's wide, flat tail is a multipurpose tool used as an efficient rudder and propeller for underwater steering and propulsion. The slap of a beaver's tail startles intruders and warns other beavers of danger. Beavers are usually nocturnal but may be seen at dawn or dusk making repairs to their lodges or dams or gathering food.

Excursions

Zealand Falls is an excellent base camp for day trips, offering perhaps the widest variety of easily accessible hikes of all the huts in the system. Outings range from casual nature walks to more demanding summit climbs.

The easy 5-mile round trip to the head of Thoreau Falls and back is a thoroughly worthwhile outing in all seasons but is especially pleasant in spring when the water is at peak flow. Pick up Ethan Pond Trail below the hut, which follows the abandoned Zealand Railroad bed and crosses the talus slope beneath the steep, fire-scarred walls of Whitewall Mountain before connecting with Thoreau Falls Trail to reach the head of the falls. There are excellent views into Zealand Notch and across the Pemigewasset Wilderness along the way.

The open ledges at Zeacliff provide a spectacular, un-impeded panorama of Zealand Notch and the great expanse of the Pemigewasset Wilderness. This 3-mile round trip ascends 1,000 feet above the hut to take in a remarkable expanse of forest that little more than a century ago had been completely denuded. Follow Twinway Trail from the hut. Allow 1 hour each way.

At 4,054 feet, Mount Hale is the second-highest peak in the vicinity of the hut. There are decent views from its summit, which once held a fire tower. Many of the rocks around the former tower are reputed to be strongly magnetic. Follow Twinway Trail from the hut for 0.1 mile to a junction with Lend-a-Hand Trail, which continues to ascend 1,300 feet over 2.6 miles to the summit. The grade is moderate, but the footing can be difficult. Allow 2 hours each way.

Access to the Hut

Difficulty: easy
Distance: 2.8 miles
Hiking time: 1.5 hours

In summer, Zealand Trail is the easiest, most popular route to Zealand Falls Hut. The trail begins at the end of Zealand Road, which leaves U.S. 302 at Zealand Campground, 2.3 miles east of Twin Mountain Village. The trail meanders through forest, meadows, and beaver ponds, with occasional mountain views, following an old railroad grade for 2.5 miles. It then joins Twinway Trail for a short, steep ascent (180 feet over 0.3 mile) to the hut. Allow 1.5 hours for the hike.

In winter, Zealand Road is closed. Parking is available across U.S. 302, 0.2 mile east of Zealand Road. This adds 3.2 miles to the trip for a total of 6 miles and an overall elevation gain of 1,100 feet. Allow a minimum of 3.5 hours to reach the hut.

The hut can also be reached via Avalon Trail and A–Z Trail from the east (AMC's Macomber Family Information Center at Crawford Depot). This route stretches 5.5 miles with an elevation gain of 2,000 feet. Allow 3.5 hours. For additional details regarding these routes, refer to AMC's *White Mountain Guide*.

Going Green at the Huts

A unique well pump near Zealand Falls Hut produces more than enough electricity to light the hut.

AMC has a long-standing commitment to using its huts, lodges, and camps as models for sustainable operations and environmental stewardship. All of the high huts are "off the grid," primarily powered by solar panels and small wind generators. Even during the busy summer season, the huts use an average of only two kilowatt-hours (2 kWh) of energy per day. By comparison, the average family uses 10 to 20 kWh per day.

Each array of the huts' photovoltaic solar panels collects up to 900 watts of electricity per day when the sun is at its peak (between 10 A.M. and 2 P.M.). The wind generators produce power when the wind blows at 8 MPH or stronger. They produce their peak of 400 watts at 28 MPH. Zealand Falls Hut also uses a unique hydropower system built by AMC's Construction Crew. The system produces more energy than the hut consumes.

Each hut has a bank of 12 to 20 deep-cycle lead-acid batteries that store energy from the wind and sun and produce direct current to power refrigerators, lights, and water pumps. The huts also use high-efficiency refrigerators designed to run off solar-powered electrical systems. The refrigerators are 10 to 15 times more efficient than typical refrigerators. Four-watt, energy-efficient compact fluorescent bulbs are used in all of the huts to provide light in the kitchens, dining rooms, and libraries. At Lonesome Lake, there is a solar-powered, hot water preheat system.

All six below-treeline huts (Lonesome Lake, Greenleaf, Galehead, Zealand Falls, Mizpah Spring, and Carter Notch) have composting toilets. Above treeline, the huts use an AMC-designed waterless storage system. These systems have reduced the amount of waste flown out at the end of the huts' full-service season.

AMC focuses on reducing waste and recycling wherever possible. Food waste is composted, and all AMC huts promote a carry-in, carry-out policy. Hut visitors can learn more about AMC's "Green Promise" by listening to one of the "green technology" talks offered daily by hut naturalists. More information can be found at www.outdoors.org/greenpromise.

8

Mizpah Spring Hut

First opened: 1965

Elevation: 3,777 feet

Coordinates: 44° 13′ 09″ N, 71° 22′ 10″ W

Location: White Mountain National Forest/shoulder of Mount Pierce overlooking the Dry River Wilderness

Sleeping capacity: 60 in 8 co-ed bunkrooms

Season: early May to mid-October (caretaker basis in May)

Green systems in use: solar panels, solar water preheat, composting toilets, food composting, and compact fluorescent lighting

Interesting fact: the only hut with an organ (but not the first!)

About the Hut

In August 1961, a comprehensive 35-page article titled "The Friendly Huts of the White Mountains" appeared in *National Geographic* magazine. At the time, the well-known periodical had a circulation approaching 7 million. The article's author, William O. Douglas, was an avid outdoorsman who also happened to be an associate justice of the U.S. Supreme Court. Complemented by dozens of full-color photographs, Douglas's article was a thorough, inviting account of the hut experience, the natural wonders of the region, and AMC's essential role in its recreational development and preservation. The resulting publicity had an immediate and profound impact on AMC's mountain refuges and largely etched AMC's resolve to build Mizpah Spring Hut.

Foot traffic to the huts, and outdoor recreation in general, had been steadily rising since the late 1950s. In fact, by the time the article appeared, the hut croos were collectively preparing nearly 45,000 meals annually. But, as one hutmaster of the era recalled it, there was a "tremendous quantum jump" in business following the article's publication. With the huts stretched to capacity, and the croos exhausted by the influx of visitors, AMC set to work to renovate or expand existing structures at Lakes of the Clouds, Carter Notch, Lonesome Lake, and Pinkham Notch. AMC collaborated with the Forest Service to find a suitable location for a new hut.

The obvious site would bridge the substantial gap between the huts at Zealand Falls and Lakes of the Clouds, which prior to Mizpah's opening required a full

Young hikers tuck in for the night in one of Mizpah's eight
cozy bunkrooms.

day of hiking over often difficult, exposed terrain. The
location would also serve as the link between the four
huts to the south and west (Lonesome, Greenleaf, Galehead, and Zealand), and AMC's original huts at Lakes,
Madison, Pinkham, and Carter. Fortunately, AMC was
able to minimize its impact by locating the new hut at
the site of its old Mizpah Spring shelter, which was
built in 1915 and had provided trampers basic refuge
for nearly five decades.

Mizpah was built to withstand 200 MPH winds and,
with its steep roofline, endure heavy snow loads. But the
hut is best appreciated from inside. Large, south-facing
windows filter ample sunlight into the dining room,
which has an expansive cathedral ceiling supported by

attractive, exposed beams. A stairway next to the front desk and kitchen leads to a long hallway with bunkrooms of varying sizes. Mizpah is also the only hut with a separate library and game room.

Visitors may be surprised to find a pump organ sitting quietly next to the bookshelf in the library. Although it no longer plays, one can imagine sonorous notes drifting through the hut while the wind danced through the treetops outside. Gracing a wall at the entrance to the kitchen is a large, iron dinner gong that is rung heartily before meals are served. Willy Ashbrook (Mizpah's first hutmaster and known for packing in heavy loads) packed the gong to the hut in 1965.

Today, after nearly a half-century, Mizpah Spring Hut remains a preferred destination for families and groups interested in exploring the alpine zone from a safe haven below timberline and for experienced hikers initiating or completing a hut-to-hut traverse of the Presidential Range. It's also a popular destination for day-trippers staying at AMC's Highland Center Lodge.

Natural History

The name *Mizpah* is thought to mean "pillar in the wilderness" or "watchtower" and is variously attributed to American Indian or Hebrew origin. Either way, it is an apt term for a hut that overlooks a vast expanse of wild, protected land. In fact, the very year Mizpah was built, President Lyndon Johnson signed the 1964 Wilderness Act into law. A decade after the hut opened, Congress employed the Act to designate the Presidential Range–Dry River Wilderness, which now protects nearly 28,000 acres a few footsteps from Mizpah's doorway.

The Dry River's headwaters flow from Oakes Gulf, a large glacial cirque south of Mount Washington. The Dry, and the Rocky Branch to the east, cut through the heart of the Wilderness, which is spectacularly framed by the Southern Presidentials to the west and the Montalban Ridge to the east. Spruce-fir vegetation runs from the river bottoms to the high ridgelines, but northern hardwoods predominate at the southern end of the range and alpine-adapted plants on the exposed ridge tops.

The wilderness is home to an array of wildlife including deer, moose, black bear, and the captivating Bicknell's thrush. This elusive songbird was first recorded in the White Mountains in 1882 and, because of its restricted habitat, is on Audubon's watch list of species among the "highest conservation concern." The Bicknell's thrush prefers to breed in the rugged, windswept mountaintops of the Northeast at elevations between 3,000 feet and 4,300 feet. In the fall, it departs for southern climes among the hilltops of the Greater Antilles, an 1,800-mile journey.

Upon its return in spring, the Bicknell's thrush exhibits a unique breeding strategy known as "female-defense polygynandry," where both males and females pair with more than one mate. During courtship, the male conducts a "chase flight" with crest raised and bill open, singing behind potential mates. The song is distinctive: four phrases with a constant or slightly rising inflection at the end. Thus wooed, the female picks a nest site at the edge of the alpine zone among the dense, weather-beaten balsam firs known as krummholz. Like Mizpah Spring Hut, the cup-shaped nest is built to withstand the elements. The outer structure is deftly constructed of twigs and moss, padded with rotting vegetation, and then lined with fine plant materials such as horsehair fungus.

Excursions

Visitors to Mizpah can enjoy fine views from two distinct and interesting 4,000-footers north or south of the hut.

At an elevation of 4,312 feet, Mount Pierce (formerly Mount Clinton) offers a sampling of the alpine zone from its rocky dome. The exposure is brief, but in poor weather the effect is quickly appreciated. Pierce was originally named after New York Governor DeWitt Clinton, a well-respected botanist and presidential candidate defeated by James Madison in 1812. A century later, the New Hampshire legislature decided to rename the peak "in honor of the fourteenth president of the United States and the only citizen or resident of New Hampshire who has been the incumbent of that exalted office." Franklin Pierce served one term from 1853 to 1857 and remains the only president from the state. Access to the summit is via Webster Cliff Trail along the AT. From the hut, the trail rises steeply and includes wooden ladders in places. The elevation gain is 500 feet. Allow one hour for the 1.6-mile round trip.

To the south, Mount Jackson's coned summit (4,052 feet) is a mere 250 feet higher than the hut. Yet the views to the southern Presidentials, Dry River Wilderness, and Montalban Ridge are spectacular, and the hike passes through interesting alpine meadows and open ledges. It's a perfect outing for younger hikers or anyone uncomfortable with the steep climb up (and down) Mount Pierce. From the hut, follow Mizpah Cutoff to its junction with Webster Cliff Trail. The round trip is 3.4 miles. Allow 2 hours.

Access to the Hut

Difficulty: moderate
Distance: 2.6 miles
Hiking time: 2 hours, 15 minutes

The quickest route to the hut is via Crawford Path (WMNF) and Mizpah Cutoff (AMC), which is the same route the croo uses to pack in supplies. The path is best accessed via Crawford Connector, which begins from a parking lot on Mount Clinton Road just north and east of the Highland Center off U.S. 302. Allow 2 hours and 15 minutes hiking time.

Alternatively, you can continue on Crawford Path beyond Mizpah Cutoff to its junction with Webster Cliff Trail (AMC), which puts you on the AT, provides excellent views of the Presidential Range, and exposes you to a small section of the alpine zone across the summit of Mount Pierce before descending sharply to the hut.

High Flying

At Carter Notch Hut, there is no clear, flat spot for the helicopter to land on the ground. Instead, there is a landing pad on the bunkhouse roof.

Supplying the high huts in advance of the busy summer season requires ample preparation and a well-organized team. In the early days, supplies were packed to the huts by men and mules, but today, AMC employs transport helicopters to haul the nearly 20,000 pounds of supplies needed to stock each hut. Everything from flour to soap, tomato puree to propane, and blankets to construction materials is airlifted to the huts each spring in a highly choreographed process—known as the spring airlift—that begins months beforehand.

In February, AMC's Storehouse Department starts purchasing food and supplies that will be delivered to the huts. The goods are stored in eight different tractor trailers, one for each hut. The process of loading the trailers takes more than a month. The Storehouse crew has to count everything delivered to Pinkham Notch and distribute the correct amount of food for each location. The trailers are then driven to the huts' respective airlift sites. Depending on the weather and the winds, the pilot and AMC crew choose which huts to fly to on a given day. A convoy of trucks meet at the airlift site with last-minute items, nets, hardware, and a lot of people to move boxes.

Two teams are staged for the airlift. The bottom crew loads nets of food and supplies, each weighing as close to the maximum transportable load (approximately 800 pounds) as possible. The top crew of 4 people are flown to the hut to receive, stack, and store the supplies. Several trips are required to complete the task for each hut. To maximize the efficient use of the helicopters, AMC uses an "in-load/out-load" process: Whenever something is flown in, it is matched with an "out-load" of empty propane cylinders, solid waste, or trash.

Helicopters were first used by AMC during the construction of Mizpah Spring Hut in 1964. They quickly proved to be much more efficient than the "donks" and caused decidedly less impact on the trails. While hut croos still carry 40 to 80 pounds of perishables per person twice a week during the summer and fall, the majority of bulk goods are left for the airlift each spring.

Lakes of the Clouds Hut

First opened: 1915

Elevation: 5,012 feet

Coordinates: 44° 15′ 32″ N, 71° 19′ 08″ W

Location: Mount Washington

Sleeping capacity: 90 in 8 co-ed bunkrooms; an emergency refuge room under the hut accommodates six backpackers

Season: early June to mid-September

Green systems in use: solar panels, solar water preheat, waterless toilets, food composting, and compact fluorescent lighting

Interesting fact: the only hut where supplies are packed *down* to the hut

About the Hut

In the croo room at Lakes of the Clouds Hut hangs a somber reminder of the tragedy that prompted AMC to establish a refuge here more than a century ago. The solemn bronze plaque reads simply, "On this spot William B. Curtis perished in the great storm of June 30, 1900." A similar plaque memorializing Allen Ormsbee, Curtis's hiking companion that day, is affixed to a stone edifice a few hundred yards short of Mount Washington's summit.

By all accounts, Curtis and Ormsbee were fit, competent men. Indeed, the report of their untimely deaths published by *The New York Times* on July 4, 1900, was headlined "Athletes Perish in Blizzard." The younger Ormsbee, 28, was a prominent athlete and businessman from Brooklyn. Curtis, 63, had founded the New York Athletic Club and was considered the patriarch of American amateur athletics after founding the Amateur Athletic Union (AAU) in 1888. Later in life, he established his favorite organization, the Fresh Air Club of New York, and turned his considerable energy toward leading extended rambles and vigorous hikes.

The pair had set out that summer morning intent on scaling the high peak to take part in AMC's annual field meeting, which was being held at the Summit House. But when they started up Crawford Path it had already turned cold, and clouds were gathering into what would later be called "the storm of the century." By the time they reached Mount Pleasant (now Mount Eisenhower) and signed the register, conditions were quickly deteriorating. They wrote, "Rain clouds and wind sixty miles—Cold."

Daily skits delivered by croo members provide essential information and playful entertainment at the high huts.

Soon the determined men passed two local guides descending the path but ignored their warnings to turn back. By the time they reached Mount Monroe, the temperature plummeted to near freezing, and the furious wind and rain were quickly melding into sheets of slippery ice. With their goal now little more than a mile away, Curtis and Ormsbee carried on.

Meanwhile atop Mount Washington, hurricane-force winds were battering the Summit House. Unable to mount a search, the AMC members inside could only hunker down and hope that the two men had either turned back or would somehow prevail.

At Lakes of the Clouds, Curtis succumbed to the unrelenting tempest. Ormsbee pushed on for help, but collapsed a few hundred yards from the signal station at the summit. The storm lasted for 60 hours.

The AMC members gathered at the summit immediately resolved to build a refuge near Crawford Path in proximity to where Curtis and Ormsbee perished. The following year, a wooden shelter was constructed "100 rods beyond the point where Mr. Curtis' body was found...." A sign placed over the door read, "Not for pleasure camping." But the shelter received heavy use nonetheless, and in time it became apparent that a larger, more substantial structure was necessary. So, in 1915, a stone hut was built, complete with kitchen and bunk space for 36.

Since then, Lakes of the Clouds Hut has gone through several renovations, including additions in 1922, 1927, 1947, 1968, and again in 2005. Today, it is AMC's largest and most popular hut and is considered the flagship facility of the system. Its eight bunkrooms can accommodate 90 guests, and a shelter beneath the hut, accessible from outside, provides refuge for six hikers in the event of an emergency.

Natural History

At 5,012 feet, Lakes of the Clouds is AMC's highest hut. Perched on a shelf at the lip of Ammonoosuc Ravine, in a low saddle between Mount Washington and Mount Monroe, the hut is an ideal location to explore the alpine zone, one of New England's rarest, most fascinating ecosystems. The celebrated alpine wildflowers that bloom here every summer have adapted to survive some of our planet's harshest conditions.

Thousands of years ago, when glaciers receded from the region, alpine tundra covered much of the Northeast. But as the climate warmed, the tundra shrank until it was largely isolated to the colder climates among the high peaks. These stranded, fragile islands are at once delicate and remarkable in their resilience and adaptation to such an extreme environment.

Here, size matters. Some of the plants are little more than an inch tall, which keeps the buds and stems sheltered from the wind. Dark leaves are adapted to absorb sunlight efficiently. As winter fades and the snow melts in mid- to late June, the colorful show begins. Diapensia emerges in dense clusters of petite white flowers, along with the larger magenta flowers of Lapland rosebay, a dwarf rhododendron. The alpine azalea appears at this time of year too, sprouting small pink flowers.

Midsummer flowers, blooming from late June into July, include the fragrant alpine marsh violet, and alpine bistort. Alpine brook saxifrage, which is relatively rare but found near Lakes of the Clouds, blooms in July and August. It produces a diminutive white flower and grows in tufts among boulders. Colorful bluebells bloom from July into September, along with mountain sandwort and, in late summer, vivid yellow alpine goldenrods. In July, mountain avens, which grows only in the White Mountains and in Nova Scotia, blooms profusely around Lakes of the Clouds. This endemic plant is fairly large by alpine standards.

New England's rarest alpine plant is the Robbins, or dwarf, cinquefoil whose five-petaled, yellow flowers bloom in early summer; it is found only on Mount Washington and along Franconia Ridge. The increase in human traffic across the fragile alpine zone following completion of Crawford Path in 1819 resulted in the plant's rapid decline. By 1980, the cinquefoil was on the brink of extinction and was placed on the endangered species list, which sparked a long-term recovery effort spearheaded by AMC, U.S. Fish and Wildlife, the New England Wildflower Society, and the White Mountain National Forest. Years of data collecting and study, seed propagation, replanting, and trail relocations resulted in the plant's successful rescue. On August 28, 2002, the cinquefoil was officially removed from the federal endangered species list.

Because of its above-treeline location near cloud cover, Lakes of the Clouds is also a focal point for AMC's air quality research. AMC began research on acid rain here in 1984 and began monitoring for fine particulates and haze in 1988. Researchers measure the concentration of small particles in the air using a particle monitor known as a Harvard Impactor. Particles are collected over a 24-hour period. The filter is then weighed and chemically analyzed to determine how much and what types of particulate matter are in the air sample.

Using such techniques, researchers have determined that visibility in the Great Gulf Wilderness is impaired by haze, primarily caused by sulfates (from coal-burning power plants). In the nine-year period from 1988 to 1996, the median summertime daily visibility in the

The area around Lakes of the Clouds Hut has been a focal point for AMC's air quality research since 1988.

Gulf was about 54 miles, compared with the natural visual range of approximately 80 to 90 miles.

Excursions

For good reason, Lakes of the Clouds is AMC's most popular hut. From its comfortable shelter, hikers can enjoy excursions to the White Mountain's most notable destinations, including the Alpine Garden Natural Area and, of course, Mount Washington.

Before European settlers arrived, New England's highest peak (6,288 feet) was called Agiocochook, or "home of the Great Spirit." It received its present name in 1784 in honor of President George Washington. Today, the mountain is home to many things, including a cog railway, auto road, observatory, restaurant, museum, and a world-renowned reputation for "the world's worst weather." In fair weather, the climb to the summit from the hut is a relatively straightforward ramble over exposed talus via Crawford Path. Allow 1.5 hours to ascend the 1,300 feet.

A visit to the Alpine Garden is well worth the trip, especially in early summer when the alpine flowers described above are in bloom. It can be accessed directly from the hut via Tuckerman Crossover Trail or combined with an ascent of Mount Washington to form a loop hike. AMC's *White Mountain Guide* provides specific trail distances and descriptions.

Another popular outing from Lakes is a leisurely 0.3-mile ascent of Mount Monroe, which rises just beyond the hut's doorstep. The summit affords fine views into Oakes Gulf, Lakes of the Clouds, and Mount Washington. This may also be combined with the Mount Monroe Loop, which crosses the summit and meets Crawford Path to form a 1.1-mile roundabout.

Access to the Hut

Difficulty: moderate
Distance: 3.1 miles
Hiking time: 3 hours

Ammonoosuc Ravine Trail is an attractive and popular pathway and is the most direct route of ascent to Lakes of the Clouds Hut. Because it is well protected much of the way, it is also the best route to or from the hut in bad weather. However, the last mile of the trail is extremely steep and rough, and it may be too strenuous for inexperienced hikers, especially on the descent. From the Base Road hiker's parking lot south of the Cog Railway Base Station, the 3.1-mile route climbs 2,500 feet to the hut (more than 1,500 feet in the last mile!). Allow nearly 3 hours to complete the trip.

The hut can also be reached via the historic Crawford Path, established in 1819 and considered the oldest continuously maintained recreational footpath in the United States. The hut is accessed from Pinkham Notch using Tuckerman Ravine Trail. From the south, the trail ascends much the same route traversed by Curtis and Ormsbee in 1900, ascending 3,450 feet over 7 miles. In good weather, plan on at least 5 hours' hiking time. Mount Washington is the northern terminus of Crawford Path, and the descent to the hut from New England's highest summit is a viable and popular route in good weather. However, the entire route is above treeline and completely exposed to the region's fierce weather. Extreme caution should be exercised at all times. The path to the hut descends 1,300 feet over 1.5 miles. Allow 45 minutes to 1 hour. Refer to AMC's *White Mountain Guide* for trail details and precautions.

Ben Campbell's Heavy Soles

The story of Ben Campbell's boots
is one of many intriguing hut legends.

Ghostly tales and unexplained phenomena swirl around
AMC's high huts. From "The Presence" at Lakes of the
Clouds to the apparition of Milton E. "Red Mac" Mac-
Gregor (huts manager in the 1920s known to pull pranks
on the croo at Carter Notch Hut), there are plentiful stories of things that go bump in the night. But none
touches the heart like the tale of Ben Campbell's boots.

Campbell joined AMC in the summer of 1977, working as a croo member at Greenleaf Hut. He loved the
work and was very much at home in the mountains. In
1978, he became assistant hutmaster at Lakes of the
Clouds Hut, and that winter he stayed on to serve as
caretaker at Carter Notch Hut. In 1979, he was selected
to be hutmaster at Greenleaf Hut. On June 13 that year,
he wrote a few thoughts in the hut's croo log:

*Already slipping into the routine of the summer,
the packing and the meals and all of the questions.
It's like the comfortable feel of an old boot.*

For the 1980 season, Campbell was chosen to become hutmaster at Lakes of the Clouds. It was the job he coveted but, tragically, one he would never fill.

On May 16, a few weeks shy of the start of the hut season, Campbell fell to his death while hiking in the Scottish Highlands. He was just 23 years old. Friends and volunteers gathered to construct paths and tent platforms along his favorite trails in his memory, and one friend handcrafted a solid oak door, which was later hung at Carter Notch Hut. To honor Campbell's love of the mountains and his joy in working at the huts, his family delivered his hiking boots to Greenleaf Hut.

But soon after, the Greenleaf croo reported hearing the thump of boots walking in the night. In the mornings, they would find Campbell's boots in a different part of the hut. Stories of these restless boots persisted until someone suggested that the shoes might not be at home at Greenleaf. After all, Campbell had been looking forward to working as hutmaster at Lakes of the Clouds. Perhaps the agitated soles were not comfortable at Greenleaf? The boots were delivered to Lakes of the Clouds Hut, where they have hung in the croo room… quietly ever since.

10
Madison Spring Hut

First opened: 1889

Elevation: 4,800 feet

Coordinates: 44° 19′ 40″ N, 71° 17′ 00″ W

Location: Northern Presidentials, between Mount Madison and Mount Adams

Sleeping capacity: 52 in 2 large, co-ed bunkrooms

Season: early June to mid-September

Green systems in use: solar panels, wind generation, waterless toilets, food composting, and compact fluorescent lighting

Interesting fact: oldest hut site in the United States

About the Hut

In February 1889, AMC members Rosewell Lawrence and Laban Watson climbed to the high col between Mounts Madison and Adams for a "dedicatory visit" to the Appalachian Mountain Club's recently built hut at Madison Spring. The previous year, AMC had resolved to build that summer "a permanent stone cabin...provided with sleeping bunks, a stove, and the most necessary furniture." One acre of land was donated to AMC for this purpose by the Brown Lumber Company, to be known as the Madison Spring Reservation (it remains in AMC ownership to this day). The hut would serve as a base for mountain exploration and provide a modicum of hospitality for hikers making the long trek to Mount Washington from the remote Northern Peaks. AMC set aside $700 to accomplish the task.

Once they arrived, the two men lit a fire in the hut's stove but promptly regretted doing so: "The thick frost on the rafters over the stove began to melt and drip...all afternoon it dripped, dripped, dripped in all parts of the hut." Despite the soggy welcome, the men's spirits did not dampen. While Lawrence, who was then AMC's recording secretary, cautioned subsequent visitors "not to expect too much," he enthusiastically concluded the hut "is a great institution; its construction is one of the best things the Club has done."

Indeed, it was. And almost immediately, the people came. This was, after all, the "Golden Age" of White Mountain resorts, and visitors were already being drawn to the mountains by the thousands. Although Madison

In summer 2010, AMC's Construction Crew embarked on a major rebuild of Madison Spring Hut while preserving its historical integrity.

was decidedly rustic by comparison to the grand hotels of the era, the hut commanded spectacular views from its lofty perch, and the trek to its doorstep was inviting to more adventurous trampers.

By 1892, "churlish" crowds were taxing the environment around the hut, cutting down nearby trees for firewood despite AMC's fervent admonitions. By 1895, AMC reports showed overcrowding to be endemic, and the hut itself was repeatedly vandalized. So in 1906, AMC responded with an ambitious expansion of the hut—doubling its capacity to 24—and an equally ambitious plan to hire a summer "care-keeper," whose salary would be offset by charging visitors a small fee. That summer, 469 guests paid 50 cents a night to stay at Madison Spring Hut.

Kenneth Swan, Madison's second hutmaster, observed that many of the clientele were ill-prepared for their adventures, and he suggested the AMC consider supplying meals for hikers. In 1911, AMC built a separate stone hut at Madison Spring to serve as a cookhouse. Meals for 428 guests were prepared the following season. By 1922, a third stone building was added, and in 1929, it was enlarged to replace the original hut.

On October 7, 1940, disaster struck. A fire erupted in the kitchen and quickly engulfed the main hut. After more than a half-century of service, Madison was no more. Again AMC responded with typical zeal and determination. With the aid of donkeys and shoulder pads borrowed from the Berlin High School football team, the crew hauled 50 tons of materials up the mountain in six weeks and went to work to build a new hut from the stone foundation that remained. Remarkably, by August 1941, Madison Hut was ready to receive guests once again with mountain hospitality.

After more than a century of service, Madison—also known as "Madhouse" or "Chez Belle"—remains one of AMC's more popular huts, and a welcome refuge for the multitudes of hikers who have enjoyed its shelter from the region's harsh alpine weather. In 2010, AMC embarked on a major rebuilding of the hut to make it more comfortable for guests and to support AMC's "Green Promise" of sustainable operations while maintaining the

Newly rebuilt Madison Spring Hut weathered its first winter in 2010.

building's historical integrity. The stone foundation was preserved, while the bunkrooms, croo quarters, and kitchen were rebuilt, and a waterless toilet system was added.

Natural History

The Northern Peaks of the White Mountains are, in many ways, as interesting as their loftier, more popular neighbor to the south. They are certainly more remote and arguably as rugged. The range runs along a crescent arc north and east from the summit of Mount Washington and overlooks the Great Gulf, the largest glacial cirque in the White Mountains.

The hut is situated at the edge of the alpine transition zone, where trees and tundra adapt to survive fierce winds and frigid winters. Spruce and balsam fir predominate, but only near rock formations where they can gain a firm foothold and a semblance of shelter. The same species might grow to 30 or 40 feet at lower elevations, but here they are stunted and deformed.

The twisted wood, known as krummholz, is a phenomenon unique to subarctic and subalpine treeline landscapes. In these environments, the trees disperse most of their energy out of harm's way, so the growth is particularly dense near the ground. Some of the krummholz formations near the hut are estimated to be almost 200 years old. Alpine plants near Madison include Diapensia, Lapland rosebay, and alpine azalea, which all bloom in late June. You'll also find mountain cranberry, Labrador tea, mountain sandwort, and mountain avens here, blooming in late July. In some places, you may observe a large green plant known as Indian poke or false hellebore.

Lichens abound too. Several species grow on the rocks surrounding the hut. Lichens are often overlooked but represent some of the oldest living organisms on earth. They like extremes and typically thrive in harsh environments. Lichens are composite organisms and require a symbiotic partnership to survive. Fungi are the dominant partner, coupled with a photosynthetic mate such as green algae or cyanobacteria. The orange sunburst lichen that sometimes grows on the rock walls of the hut uses nutrients found in the mortar.

Lichen species at Madison include cup lichen, snow lichen, map lichen, and reindeer moss lichen. A single map lichen, grown to less than half an inch in diameter, may be more than a thousand years old!

Excursions

From the hut's doorstep there are exceptional opportunities for exploration and discovery.

At 5,799 feet, Mount Adams is New England's second highest peak and is by far the most interesting in the region. It has magnificent views from its classic, conical summit, two inspiring ridges, four minor peaks, and five glacial cirques. To enjoy it all, consider a loop hike beginning with an interesting, sometimes steep, scramble to the summit via Star Lake Trail. The trail's namesake is a beautiful, boggy tarn, arguably one of the most picturesque mountain ponds in the White Mountains. It was so named by 19th guidebook writer Moses Sweetser, "on account of its extreme height and because it mirrors so perfectly the constellations above."

From Adam's summit, pick up Air Line Trail to Gulfside Trail for the return to the hut. The junction of these two trails puts you at the lip of King Ravine, a classic, U-shaped glacial cirque with its deep, broad valley and near-vertical sidewalls. Looking northward, the wide ridge to the west is Nowell. The narrow, "knife-edged" ridge to the east is Durand.

Mount Madison is the northernmost peak of the Presidential Range and provides a less rigorous but equally enjoyable day trip. The summit rises 500 feet from the hut over 0.5 mile. There are fine views in all directions from the rocky summit, especially south and southeast to the Great Gulf and Mount Washington. Outside of Katahdin, Madison is the largest mountain in New England in proximity to a major river. From the east and northeast, the mountain drops 4,580 feet over 6.5 miles to Androscoggin River below.

Access to the Hut

Difficulty: moderate
Distance: 3.8 miles
Hiking time: 3 hours, 40 minutes

Valley Way Trail provides the most direct access to Madison Spring Hut and is the best route of ascent or descent during inclement weather. Although the grade is relatively moderate, there are steeper pitches near the trail's end, so it manages to gain 3,550 feet in elevation over 3.8 miles. This is the same route the croo uses to pack in supplies, and they consider it the most difficult trail of all the huts to shuttle their loads. Allow 3 hours and 40 minutes for the climb.

Air Line Trail provides a more scenic alternative to Valley Way Trail, with magnificent views of King Ravine along Durand Ridge. It departs from the same parking lot as Valley Way and is nearly identical in length, duration, and elevation gain. However, it is much steeper in places, is extremely exposed along the knife edge of Durand Ridge, and should only be attempted by fit hikers in fair weather.

From the east, Madison is best approached from Daniel Webster–Scout Trail combined with either Osgood Trail or Parapet Trail from Osgood Junction. The latter avoids the summit of Mount Madison but passes by beautiful Star Lake en route to the hut. Allow at least 4 hours and 30 minutes for either option. Consult AMC's *White Mountain Guide* for details and descriptions.

The Trail Crew

AMC's Trail Crew, shown here operating a griphoist highline system, transports heavy rocks in the alpine zone.

When AMC was established in 1876, there were fewer than a dozen paths to major summits in the White Mountains. That year, AMC hired Charles Lowe to build its first trail, a path toward the summit of Mount Adams. AMC now maintains nearly 350 miles of trails in the region, as well as several backcountry campsites. With the support of a cadre of dedicated volunteers, much of that work falls on the shoulders of the hardworking, highly skilled team of men and women of AMC's Trail Crew.

Founded in 1919, AMC's Trail Crew is among the oldest professional trail crews in the nation. In the early days, the crew was primarily focused on maintenance to established trails. But the backpacking boom of the 1960s caused a rapid increase in soil compaction and erosion. The crew quickly turned its attention to reconstruction projects utilizing new techniques—from switchbacks to advanced drainage systems—to avert further destruction. In the 1970s, the crew's focus on conservation and restoration resulted in the installation of low rock walls along Franconia Ridge to protect the fragile alpine plants near the heavily used trail. These so-called "scree walls" were initially viewed by some as "unnatural," but they are now seen as essential tools for restoration.

Today, AMC's Trail Crew is widely recognized as *the* pioneer in the art of path building, trail maintenance, and conservation. Indeed, *AMC's Complete Guide to Trail Building and Maintenance*, now in its 4th edition, is considered the definitive resource for trail work.

Carter Notch Hut

First opened: 1914

Elevation: 3,288 feet

Coordinates: 44° 15′ 33″ N, 71° 11′ 43″ W

Location: Carter Notch between Wildcat Mountain and Carter Dome

Sleeping capacity: 40 in 2 bunkhouses with rooms for 4 or 6

Season: year-round (full service in summer and early fall, self service in late fall, winter, and spring)

Green systems in use: solar panels, wind generation, composting toilets, food composting, and compact fluorescent lighting

Interesting fact: oldest hut structure in the system still in use

About the Hut

Visitors to Carter Notch, AMC's easternmost hut, will discover some of the finest scenery in the White Mountains. The hut is tucked into a secluded chasm between the steep cliffs of Wildcat Mountain and Carter Dome, amid a wild heap of immense boulders and two beautiful glacial tarns. It also lies at the western edge of the newly designated Wild River Wilderness, which encompasses nearly 24,000 acres between Carter Dome and the Baldface Range. Carter is a favorite destination for hikers, skiers, and snowshoers who enjoy the solitude and rugged splendor of a backcountry excursion.

AMC built its first shelter in Carter Notch, a small log cabin, in 1904. It served its purpose well for the next decade, but AMC's mission was quickly evolving during the period, and the notion of an "Alps-style" hut-to-hut system was already under consideration. AMC member Harvey Newton Shepard had studied the huts operated by various European clubs and recommended "a few additional huts be constructed, with good paths thereto, so that an interesting walk of three to seven days may be made without the encumbrance of the carrying of blankets or provisions. This will not only make the White Mountains better known but also is the kind of public work in which the Club should engage."

So in 1914, AMC built a more substantial stone shelter at Carter, similar to the hut at Madison Spring. The following year, AMC built a stone hut at Lakes of the

A hiker takes a welcome break from a windy day, utilizing the hut's information resources to plan her hike.

Clouds, which replaced the shelter erected there in 1901. Together, the three huts completed Shepard's vision of a triangle of accessible shelters. "They throw open, as never before, the summits of the great range and the little traversed wilderness to the east of Washington," he wrote. "A tramper can be entirely independent of hotels and good clothes and he may start with one lunch and extra clothing and be free of tents, frypans, grub bags, and endless and weighty things which usually delight to follow along with one. Tramping clothes and a cheerful spirit are the really only necessary things."

Nearly a century later, that vision and the stone hut at Carter Notch are still intact. Indeed, the hut is the oldest building still in use in the system. The shelter was expanded in 1930 to add croo quarters, and three more buildings were added in 1962, including two detached bunkhouses and a wash house. In 1990, the main hut was remodeled again to update and improve the kitchen. And in 1995, a well was drilled into the side of Wildcat Mountain to provide safe drinking water for visitors. The stone hut now serves as the kitchen and dining room, and collectively, the bunkhouses can accommodate up to 40 overnight guests, with rooms for 4 or 6.

Today, the hut complex at Carter Notch is an enjoyable, all-season destination for "unencumbered trampers" and the anchor point for ambitious hikers engaging in what is now a nearly 52-mile hut-to-hut traverse from or to Lonesome Lake Hut.

Carter was first opened for winter visitors in 1972 and remains a popular destination for skiers and snowshoers during the cold season.

Natural History

It's uncertain who first coined the term "notch," but in New England the name stuck and is applied to most of the steep-sided glacial clefts (Crawford, Pinkham, Franconia, etc.) for which the region is famous. Elsewhere, the same geologic phenomenon may be called a "gap," "pass," "saddle," or "col." Notches are often found just above the source of a river.

Carter Notch is an excellent example of how glaciers scoured and carved these U-shaped valleys during their retreat at the end of the ice age 14,000 years ago. Here, the ice sheet also ripped away huge hunks of rock from the upper slopes of Wildcat Mountain and Carter Dome and stacked them in a motley heap on the valley floor a thousand feet below. The boulder pile, now called the Ramparts, forms a natural wall that completely encloses the two Carter lakes, forcing the outlet brook on the south side underground. Some of the boulders in the Ramparts are so large they form small caves where ice can be found well into early summer (in the early days, the caves served as a convenient cold storage for perishables such as butter and cheese). The lingering ice releases cold air and, consequently, slows down the growing season on the scant soil nearby. As a result, the growing season in the notch is shorter, and the plants are generally smaller than they would be otherwise.

The two tarns at Carter Notch are remarkably clear. Both are oligotrophic, meaning they lack sufficient nutrients to support much plant growth and, consequently, animal life. Yet, they support a healthy population of brook trout, which are stocked here each spring by the New Hampshire Department of Fish & Game. The fish survive by eating aquatic insects that linger on the lakes' surfaces, feeding on plant debris deposited from the surrounding forest.

Carter Notch also offers a glimpse of the spruce-fir zone, where balsam fir and white birch abound. In summer, the area boasts a display of painted trillium flowers.

Excursions

Visitors to Carter will want to investigate the phenomenal talus rock pile known as the Ramparts. It is easily accessed via a side path off Wildcat River Trail 100 yards from the hut. The boulder caves invite exploration, and from the top of the heap there are good views toward Jackson. Remember to stay on the trail for both your safety and the protection of the fragile vegetation of the Ramparts.

Wildcat Mountain rises 1,200 feet above the hut and makes for a steep but enjoyable climb with excellent views overlooking the notch from a spur path just beyond the summit proper. Wildcat actually has numerous summits strung along its ridge, but A Peak, which is closest to the hut, is the highest of the lot, topping out at 4,422 feet (D Peak is the summit nearest to the Wildcat Ski Area). Pick up Wildcat Ridge Trail from Nineteen-Mile Brook Trail 0.2 mile from the hut. The round-trip distance is approximately 1.8 miles. Allow at least 1 hour.

Carter Dome (4,832 feet) and Mount Hight (4,675 feet) are reached via Carter–Moriah Trail 0.1 mile from the hut. The Dome, which forms the eastern flank of Carter Notch, once bore a fire tower and has good views from outlook ledges along the path and limited views

Hikers clamber through the boulder field just outside the bunkhouse at Carter Notch Hut.

from the summit. The trail climbs steeply out of the notch and soon reaches a spur trail to Pulpit Rock, a massive boulder that juts out over the notch, providing a spectacular outlook to the valley below. The bare summit of Mount Hight, 0.8 mile beyond Carter Dome, provides spectacular 360-degree views and the finest panorama of the Presidential Range in the region. Trip distance from the hut to Mount Hight's summit is 2.1

This Carter Notch Hut visitor enjoys a swim in one of the two mountain tarns near the hut.

miles with an elevation gain of 1,700 feet. Allow at least 3.5 hours for the round trip.

Access to the Hut

Difficulty: moderate
Distance: 3.8 miles
Hiking time: 3 hours

Nineteen-Mile Brook Trail is the easiest route to the hut and, consequently, the most popular. The trail runs from N.H. 16 about 1.0 mile north of Mount Washington

Auto Road. The trail climbs 2,000 feet over 3.8 miles. The path ascends moderately for much of the way (making it a viable route in winter for cross-country skiers) but ascends more steeply toward the height of land over the last half-mile and then drops sharply to the hut at 3.6 miles. Allow about 3 hours' hiking time.

The hut can also be reached via the spectacular but arduous Wildcat Ridge Trail (part of the AT), which can be picked up via Lost Pond Trail directly from AMC's Pinkham Notch Visitor Center. The path climbs and traverses the numerous summits along the expansive ridge of Wildcat Mountain with outstanding views of Mount Washington and into Carter Notch. Hikers should be aware that this is a steep, rough outing with numerous climbs and descents and should be avoided in poor weather or when the trail is wet or icy (see AMC's *White Mountain Guide* for more details). From Pinkham Notch Visitor Center, the route runs 5.8 miles to Nineteen-Mile Brook Trail with an elevation gain of 3,150 feet (and descents amounting to 1,050 feet). Allow a minimum of 4.5 hours for this stretch. From there, Nineteen-Mile Brook Trail descends sharply over 0.2 mile to the hut.

Log On

Each hut has a library of logbooks that provide a fascinating account of visitors' experiences.

Got up this morning.... Cold, and I mean good and cold. About 40 below. The wind is blowing something awful!
> Anonymous
> Galehead Hut Log—November 1939

The human impulse to record our adventures is as old as time itself. With hands cupped to our mouths, we shout from the mountaintop: *I was here!* The urge is at once private and social, an exclamation of our unique experience, and an invitation to share it with others.

I knew there were boys up here. That's why I came.
> Kathy Golden
> Madison Spring Hut Log—July 1964

For visitors to the high huts, this impulse to record has been documented in AMC's registers and logbooks for more than a century. Most huts have 30 to 40 years of logbooks on hand. Older logs are archived at AMC's library in Boston.

I am having a new 50 star flag flown over the Supreme Court Building, Wash. DC on July 4, 1960 and sending it to Madison Hut in appreciation of the wonderful hospitality of the crew on my visit here.

William O. Douglas
Madison Spring Hut Log—June 1960

Often, the record is simply a date and signature, the modern equivalent of carving one's initials in a tree. Sometimes, there are artful renderings of life on the trail. Occasionally, eloquent reflections of the mountain experience.

First hike ever—very challenging. Huts and crew were a blessing! Thank you & God for this wonderful adventure. The mountains are truly majestic.

Summit Sista' Mary Nurge
Greenleaf Hut Log—September 2001

Appendix A

Timeline of AMC's Hut System

1876 AMC founded in Boston by MIT professor Edward Pickering and a small group of outdoor enthusiasts for the purpose of exploration, scientific investigation, and preservation of New Hampshire's high peaks.

1877 Dr. William Gray Nowell, AMC's first councillor of improvements, proposes building an alpine hut—similar to mountain refuges seen in Europe—to shelter hikers exploring the White Mountains.

1888 Formal proposal is made at AMC's 93rd corporate meeting to build a permanent stone cabin at Madison Spring in the saddle between Mount Adams and Mount Madison; $700 budgeted to accomplish the task.

1889 In February, the modest, somewhat damp hut receives its first "Dedicatory Visit." The subsequent report proclaims Madison "one of the best things the Club has done" but also advises future visitors "not to expect too much."

1901   In response to the deaths of two hikers caught in a violent storm attempting to reach AMC's annual field meeting atop Mount Washington, AMC builds an emergency refuge near Lakes of the Clouds.

1904   First shelter at Carter Notch built, a small log cabin.

1906   Madison Spring Hut expanded; first "care-keeper" hired to maintain the hut.

1911   A second building added at Madison Spring to provide space for cooking and serving meals. Original building becomes the dormitory.

1914   New, stone hut built at Carter Notch to replace log cabin. Still in use today, the stone hut is the oldest hut building in the system.

1915   Lakes of the Clouds Hut built near Crawford Path to replace older shelter.

1916   A guide to AMC's huts lists lodging rates at 75 cents per night, with meals provided by caretakers also at 75 cents each.

1920   Original log cabins built at Pinkham Notch, establishing North Country base of operations.

1922   A third structure built at Madison Spring to house more bunks in response to the hut's growing popularity. An addition built at Lakes of the Clouds, doubling its size. Joe Dodge hired as hutmaster at Pinkham Notch.

1925 Improvements made at Pinkham Notch, including new sleeping quarters.

1926 Pinkham Notch opened year-round.

1927 Pinkham Notch updated to enlarge cookhouse. Another addition made to Lakes of the Clouds to accommodate growing number of visitors.

1928 Joe Dodge becomes manager of entire hut system.

1929 State of New Hampshire purchases Franconia Notch, asks AMC to manage Lonesome Lake cabins. Greenleaf Hut built on shoulder of Mount Lafayette. Madison structures updated.

1931 Zealand Falls and Galehead built, completing a western division of huts.

1934 Pinkham Notch Lodge built to accommodate increasing number of skiers. Original log cabins combined to establish Pinkham Notch Trading Post.

1938 Ferocious hurricane levels trees around Galehead Hut, but the hut survives the storm.

1940 Kitchen fire destroys Madison Spring Hut.

1941 Construction of new hut at Madison Spring completed.

1947 Lakes of the Clouds Hut updated to enlarge kitchen, install flush toilets, and add croo quarters. Dormitory wing added to Pinkham Notch Lodge.

1959   Joe Dodge retires from AMC.

1961   Supreme Court Justice William O. Douglas writes an article about his 1960 trip to the huts for *National Geographic* magazine. Publicity generates a dramatic increase in visitors to the huts.

1962   Three more buildings added at Carter Notch.

1964–1965   Mizpah Spring Hut built in response to surge in backcountry visitors, replacing old shelter. Mizpah provides final link connecting chain of huts from west to east. Lonesome Lake Hut demolished, new facility constructed.

1968   Joe Dodge Lodge built at Pinkham Notch.

1972   Carter Notch Hut opened for winter.

1973   Zealand Falls Hut opened for winter.

1979   Lonesome Lake Hut becomes home of first all-female hut croo. Facility turned over to AMC by state of New Hampshire.

1983   Barbara Wagner becomes first female hut manager.

1988   AMC celebrates 100 years of the hut system.

1989   Greenleaf Hut expanded to enhance comfort and capacity.

1990   Carter Notch Hut updated to improve kitchen.

1995   Carter Notch Hut switched to summer self service based on interest in a lower-cost summer hut experience.

1999   White Mountain National Forest grants new 30-year special use permit for operating hut system and Pinkham Notch Visitor Center.

1999   Naturalist added to each summer hut croo.

2000   Newly rebuilt Galehead Hut opens.

2003   AMC opens Highland Center at Crawford Notch, at site of old Crawford Hostel and, previously, the Crawford House.

2005   AMC begins alpine plant monitoring program.

2007   Carter Notch Hut returned to summer and fall full service due to a dramatic dropoff in visitors during its self-service period.

2010–2011   Madison Spring Hut rebuilt with new dining room, kitchen, waterless toilets, and alternative energy systems.

Appendix B
A Day in the Life

A summer job in the White Mountains is a pretty good gig; however, for AMC's hut croos, the high mountain life isn't all play. From preparing hearty meals to stirring compost, croo members have a diverse range of duties and the tall task of carrying on a century-long tradition of providing exceptional high mountain hospitality.

The standard work schedule is 11 days at the hut and 3 days off. Each croo rotates cooking and packing duties so that during an 11-day stretch, a croo member will cook at least 4 meals and pack in supplies at least twice.

Here's a glance at the croo's daily routine, from the official croo manual:

Morning Duties

5:00 A.M.   Wake up for cook of the day. Grab an apron and prep kitchen for breakfast.

5:50 A.M.   Make early-riser coffee. Make lots and make it strong and good.

6:15 A.M.   Wake up rest of croo with music, singing, poetry...

6:30 A.M. Wake up guests with music, singing, poetry…

6:40 A.M. Prepare breakfast (oatmeal, eggs, pancakes, coffee cake, etc.).

6:45 A.M. Make more coffee!

7:00 A.M. Read weather forecast from Mount Washington Observatory; relay trip-planning and safety considerations for the day ahead.

7:00 A.M. Serve breakfast.

7:30 A.M. Perform BFD (blanket folding demonstration) and Junior Naturalist graduation ceremony

7:50 A.M. Make morning radio call to Pinkham Notch Visitor Center.

8:10 A.M. Clean up! Wash dishes, clean kitchen, and clean hut.

Daily Duties (6:30 A.M. to 9:30 P.M.)

- Record daily statistics, respond to radio calls, announce and post the weather report, giving trail and safety advice pertinent to current or upcoming conditions.
- Thoroughly clean the hut.
- Provide information on backcountry travel, natural history, trail advice, AMC programs, and facilities.

- Prepare wholesome, tasty meals served hot, on time, and in sufficient quantities.
- Wash dishes and maintain all kitchen facilities.
- Maintain all hut systems, including daily walk-through of gray water system and composting toilets; food composting; solar, wind, and hydro systems; and water pump.
- Pack finances, recyclables, and trash from the hut to the trailheads, and carry new paperwork and fresh food to the hut on Wednesdays and Saturdays.
- Conduct scheduled inventories of food, supplies, and OTC (over-the-counter) items.
- Voluntarily participate in search-and-rescue operations.

Evening Duties

5:00 P.M. Start dinner prep (make salads, set tables, cook pasta, etc.).

5:00 P.M. Give Green Technology talk and Mountain Watch talk for guests.

6:00 P.M. Serve dinner!

7:00 P.M. Give dinner talk, including the rules of the hut, opportunities (Mountain Watch Program, Junior Naturalist Program, ways to get involved with the hut, hut and hiking safety, library use, etc.), and croo introductions.

8:00 P.M.   Deliver evening interpretative programs (e.g., mountain weather, alpine ecology, White Mountain geology, fir waves).

9:00 P.M.   Prep for next day's breakfast (mix dry ingredients for bread or pancakes, crack eggs, fill water pots, defrost meat, etc.).

9:30 P.M.   Lights out!

Get into bed, and relax. You're finished…good work!

Appendix C

Mount Vernacular: A Brief Guide to High Hut Speak

Visitors to AMC's high huts are likely to stumble upon an unfamiliar word or two written in the hut logs or spoken by the croo. Like most long-standing institutions, the huts have acquired a rich lexicon of unique slang. Here are a few of the more common terms:

BFD   Blanket Folding Demonstration. A fun skit performed by the croo every morning to show guests how to fold blankets, pack out trash, and stay on the trail.

BVS   Before Vibram Soles. The time period when most hutmen wore hobnail boots.

Bull Cook   The croo member at Lakes of the Clouds Hut who attends to visitors' needs (checking them in, answering questions, providing trail information, etc.) so the kitchen cook can focus on cooking for 90 guests.

Cakers   Breakfast pancakes served up by the croo.

Cata   Nickname for Carter Notch Hut.

CC   AMC Construction Crew.

Century   A 100-pound (or more) load, packed to a hut by a croo member.

Chez Belle   Nickname for Madison Spring Hut.

Da Croo   Traditional name and spelling for AMC's hut crews (of unknown origin).

Days   Days off from the hut (croos work for 11 days straight and then have 3 days off).

Donks   Nickname for the donkeys used by AMC from 1929 to 1964 to haul materials and provisions to the high huts.

Flea   Nickname for Greenleaf Hut.

Gaboon   Pit where food waste was dumped in the early days of the huts (prior to composting and "carry-in/carry-out" methods of disposal).

Gas Bombs   Propane tanks stored on the "bomb rack" used to supply the stoves, ovens, and water heaters with propane.

Ghoul   Nickname for Galehead Hut because Huck Sharp, hutmaster in from 1934 to 1939, found a human skull (affectionately known as "Daid Haid") in one of the abandoned Pemigewasset logging camps. The skull was ultimately "retired" after it was wrapped as a wedding gift for Joe Dodge's daughter!

Goat   Food scraps.

Gorm Bucket   Bucket that holds the food scraps not eaten by guests.

Hutmen F   A term used when referring to female crew workers, before they were officially recognized as croo.

Hut Traverse   A 52-mile hike from Carter Notch Hut to Lonesome Lake Hut achieved in less than 24 hours. (The current croo record is reputedly just over 12 hours!)

Krump   To rest while packing, on a perfectly situated "krump rock."

Lakes   Nickname for Lakes of the Clouds Hut.

Lakes of the Crowds   Nickname for Lakes of the Clouds Hut on a busy summer day!

Leaf   Another nickname for Greenleaf Hut.

Madfest   A midsummer celebration held at Madison Spring Hut for all hut croos to thank them for their hard work and to promote hut system morale.

Madhaus   Nickname for Madison Spring Hut.

OH   The association of "Old Hutmen and Hutwomen" who have worked in the huts.

Pah   Nickname for Mizpah Spring Hut.

Porky Gulch   Joe Dodge's name for the original cabins at Pinkham Notch, which he frequently shared with porcupines!

Powder Monkeys   Term used by Joe Dodge when referring to the dynamite specialists who blasted new trails and sites during the construction of new huts in 1929–1931.

Poop Deck   Area where food and supplies are stored at the huts (typically the attic; named after the poop deck on a ship).

Prons   Time when the croo can take their aprons off after completing breakfast or dinner duties.

Raid   A long-standing prank of a hut croo visiting another hut (often in the middle of the night) with the goal of taking prized "raid items."

Ream   To clean thoroughly (e.g., kitchen, bathroom, croo room, oven).

Req   Requisition for fresh food and supplies that is sent to Pinkham Notch Visitor Center twice a week.

Round House   Nickname for Lonesome Lake Hut.

Sammy   Traditional hot water pot with spigot used by croo (named after the Samovar Company).

Tramper(s)   Common name for hiker(s) during the late nineteenth and early twentieth centuries.

Wake up   A musical performance by the croo at 6:30 A.M. to wake guests for breakfast.

Zool   Nickname for Zealand Falls Hut.

Appendix D
Suggested Reading

The historical information cited in this book was mainly derived from AMC's rich archive of materials and writings housed in AMC's library at 5 Joy St., Boston, MA, and/or online at www.outdoors.org. Other sources of information were drawn from a host of publications both in and out of print. The following list may provide readers additional resources to further explore topics of interest discussed in the pages of this book:

Bell, Allison, and Nancy Slack. *AMC Field Guide to the New England Alpine Summits, 2nd edition.* Boston, MA: AMC Books, 2006.

Bennett, Randall H. *The White Mountains: Alps of New England.* Mount Pleasant, SC: Arcadia Publishing, 2003.

Brown, Rebecca A. *Women on High: Pioneers of Mountaineering.* Boston, MA: AMC Books, 2002.

Daniell, Gene, and Steven D. Smith, eds. *White Mountain Guide: Hiking Trails in the White Mountain National Forest, 28th edition.* Boston, MA: AMC Books, 2007.

Grove, Bill. *J.E. Henry's Logging Railroads: The History of the East Branch & Lincoln, and Zealand Valley Railroads.* Littleton, NH: Bondcliff Books, 1998.

Hession, John, and Valerie Michaud. *Wildflowers of the White Mountains.* Burlington, VT: Huntington Graphics, 2003.

Howe, Nicholas. *Not Without Peril: 150 Years of Misadventure on the Presidential Range New Hampshire, Tenth Anniversary Edition.* Boston, MA: AMC Books, 2009.

Jarvis, Kimberly A. *Franconia Notch and the Women Who Saved It.* Lebanon, NH: University of New Hampshire Press, 2007.

Marchand, Peter J. *Nature Guide to the Northern Forest.* Boston, MA: AMC Books, 2010.

Monkman, Jerry, and Marcy Monkman. *AMC's Discover the White Mountains, 2nd edition.* Boston, MA: AMC Books, 2009.

Staff of AMC's Trails Department. *AMC's Complete Guide to Trail Building and Maintenance, 4th edition.* Boston, MA: AMC Books, 2008.

Pope, Ralph. *Lichens above Treeline: A Hiker's Guide to Alpine Zone Lichens of the Northeastern United States.* Lebanon, NH: University Press of New England, 2005.

Reifsnyder, William E. *High Huts of the White Mountains: Nature Walks, Natural History, and Day Hikes around the*

AMC's Mountain Hostels, 2nd edition. Boston, MA: AMC Books, 1994.

Stewart, Chris, and Mike Torrey, eds. *A Century of Hospitality in High Places: The Appalachian Mountain Club Hut System 1888–1988*. Boston, MA: The Appalachian Mountain Club, 1988.

Stott, Fred. *On and Off the Trail: Seventy Years with the Appalachian Mountain Club*. Boston, MA: AMC Books, 2004.

Sweetser, Moses Foster. *The White Mountains: A Handbook For Travellers* (sic). Boston, MA: Ticknor and Company, 1876.

Wroth, Katherine, ed. *White Mountain Guide: A Centennial Retrospective*. Boston, MA: AMC Books, 2007.

About the Author

Ty Wivell is an avid outdoor enthusiast who has been exploring the wilds of New England for nearly two decades. He is the author of AMC's *Discover Maine*, and works as a freelance writer, photographer, and manufacturer's representative in the outdoor industry.

Image and Design Credits

Cover design by Gia Giasullo/Studio eg

Interior design by Amanda Sylvester/Abella Publishing Services, LLC

Front cover image © Appalachian Mountain Club, originally published in 1951, artist anonymous

Back cover image by Ty Wivell, © Appalachian Mountain Club

Interior images on pages 24, 34, 37, 39, 44, 61, 65, 68, 70, 73, 80, 83, 87, 90, 92, 95, 114 by Ty Wivell, © Appalachian Mountain Club; iv, 25, 32, 35, 47, 49, 53, 58, 59, 71, 81, 93, 102, 104, 105 © Appalachian Mountain Club; 5, 6, 8, 18, 56 courtesy of AMC Archives; 11, 22, 78, 97 © Eric Pedersen; 14 © Anastasia Roy; 15 © Jerry and Marcy Monkman, ecophotography.com; 27 © Robert Kozlow; 46 by Lori Duff, © Appalachian Mountain Club; 107, 111, 112 by Herb Swanson, © Appalachian Mountain Club

AMC Hut Stamps –
Collect Them All!

Have you experienced a "wake up"?
Eaten a caker? Met the bull cook? Then you may be
eligible for a **free commemorative patch**!

tay at all eight of AMC's high huts in the White Mountains and have
his book stamped during each visit. On your last trip, the hut croo
vill verify your journey so that you can receive AMC's limited-edition
ligh Hut Patch.

Vhether you're an AMC member or simply an outdoor enthusiast, you
an take part in this hut-to-hut adventure challenge. All you need
o participate is your copy of *Passport to AMC's High Huts in the White
Mountains*!

Lakes of the Clouds Hut

JUL 31

elevation
5,012 feet

Appalachian Mountain Club

Steeped in more than 100 years of
tradition, the AMC's network of mountain
huts provides a unique backcountry
adventure for novice and experienced
hikers alike. Our huts offer mountain
hospitality in spectacular locations. Each
stay includes breakfast, dinner, and
evening program.

**For reservations call 603-466-2727
or visit www.outdoors.org/lodging.**

Appalachian Mountain Club

Founded in 1876, the AMC is the nation's oldest outdoor recreation and conservation organization. The AMC promotes the protection, enjoyment, and understanding of the mountains, forests, waters, and trails of the Appalachian region.

People
We are more than 100,000 members, advocates, and supporters; 16,000 volunteers; and more than 450 full-time and seasonal staff. Our 12 chapters reach from Maine to Washington, D.C.

Outdoor Adventure and Fun
We offer more than 8,000 trips each year, from local chapter activities to major excursions worldwide, for every ability level and outdoor interest—from hiking and climbing to paddling, snowshoeing, and skiing.

Great Places to Stay
We host more than 140,000 guests each year at our lodges, huts, camps, shelters, and campgrounds. Each AMC destination is a model for environmental education and stewardship.

Opportunities for Learning
We teach people the skills to be safe outdoors and to care for the natural world around us through programs for children, teens, and adults, as well as outdoor leadership training.

Caring for Trails
We maintain more than 1,500 miles of trails throughout the Northeast, including nearly 350 miles of the Appalachian Trail in five states.

Protecting Wild Places
We advocate for land and riverway conservation, monitor air quality and climate change, and work to protect alpine and forest ecosystems throughout the Northern Forest and Mid-Atlantic Highlands regions.

Engaging the Public
We seek to educate and inform our own members and an additional 2 million people annually through AMC Books, our website, our White Mountain visitor centers, and AMC destinations.

Join Us!
Members support our mission while enjoying great AMC programs, our award-winning *AMC Outdoors* magazine, and special discounts. Visit www.outdoors.org or call 800-372-1758 for more information.

APPALACHIAN MOUNTAIN CLUB
Recreation • Education • Conservation
www.outdoors.org